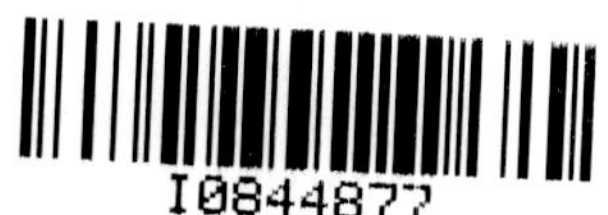

This Book Belongs To

TEST COLOR PAGE

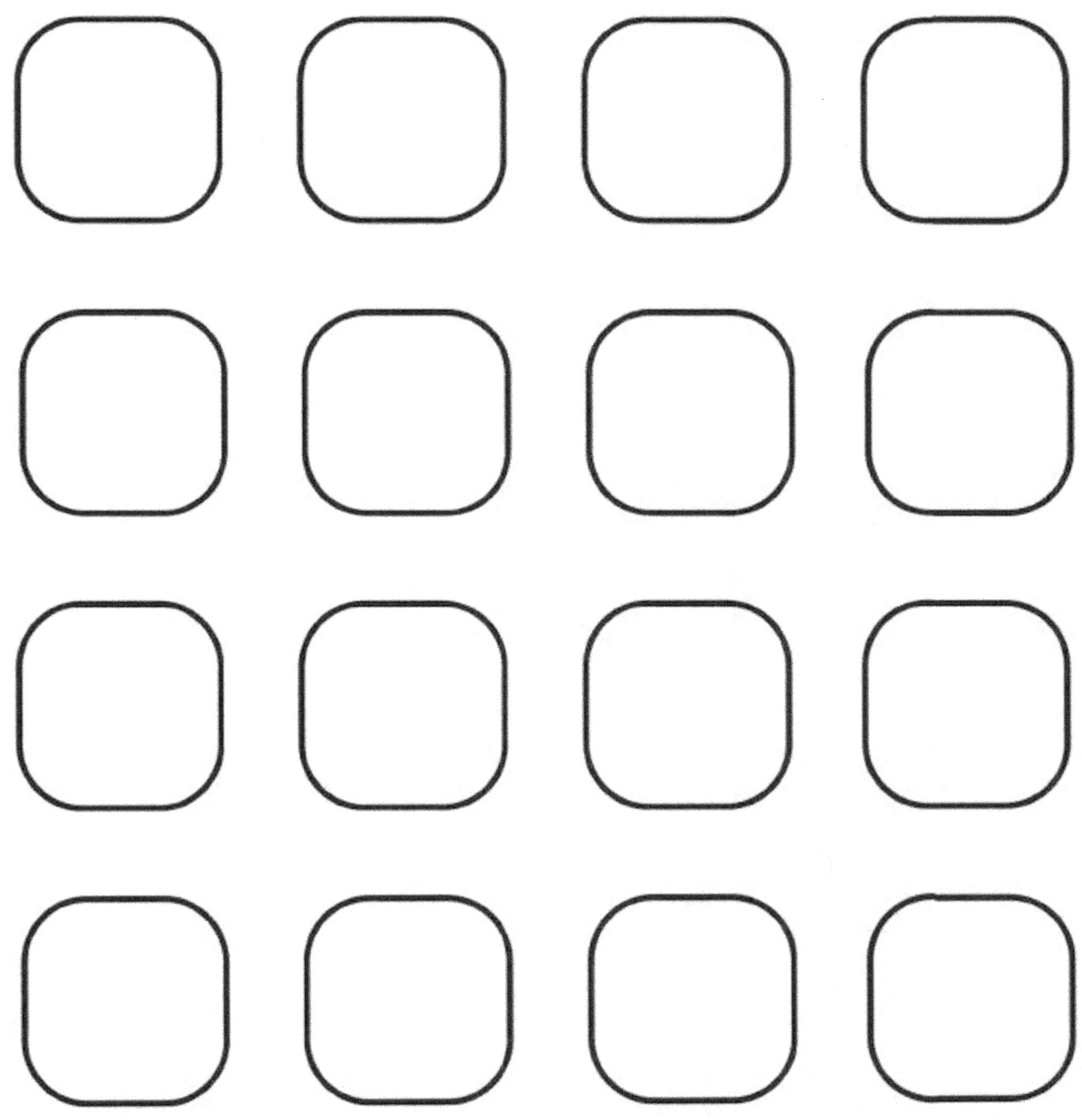

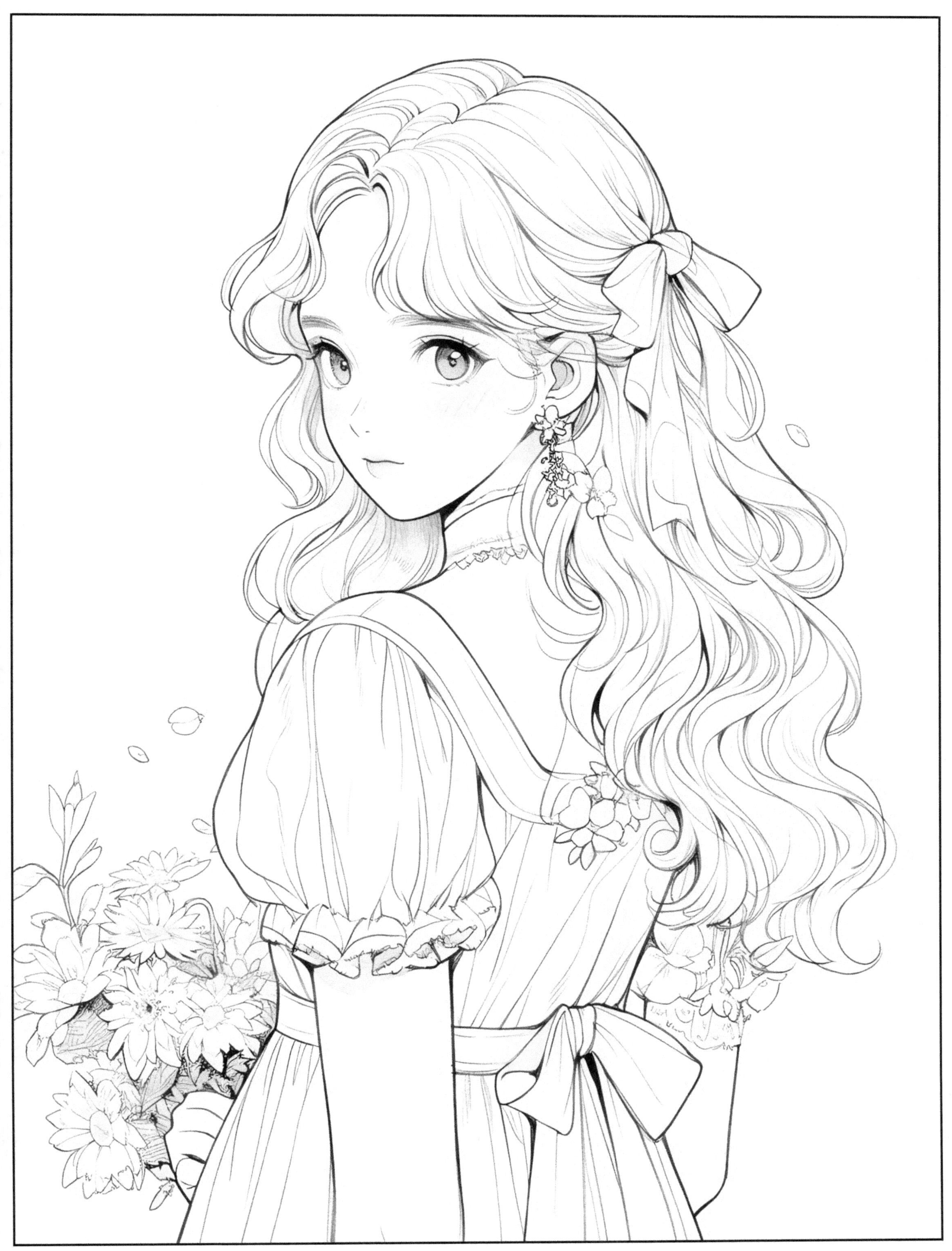

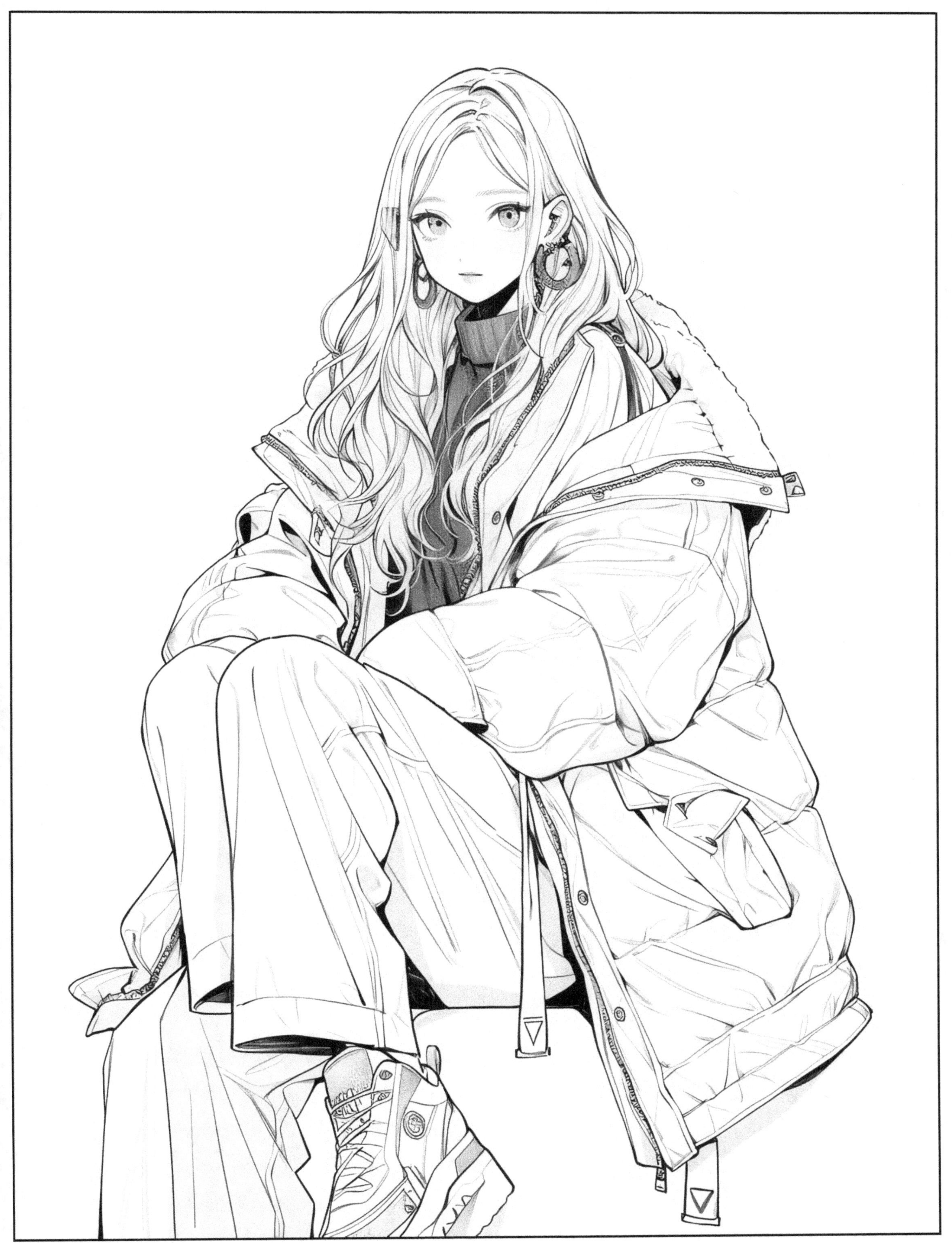

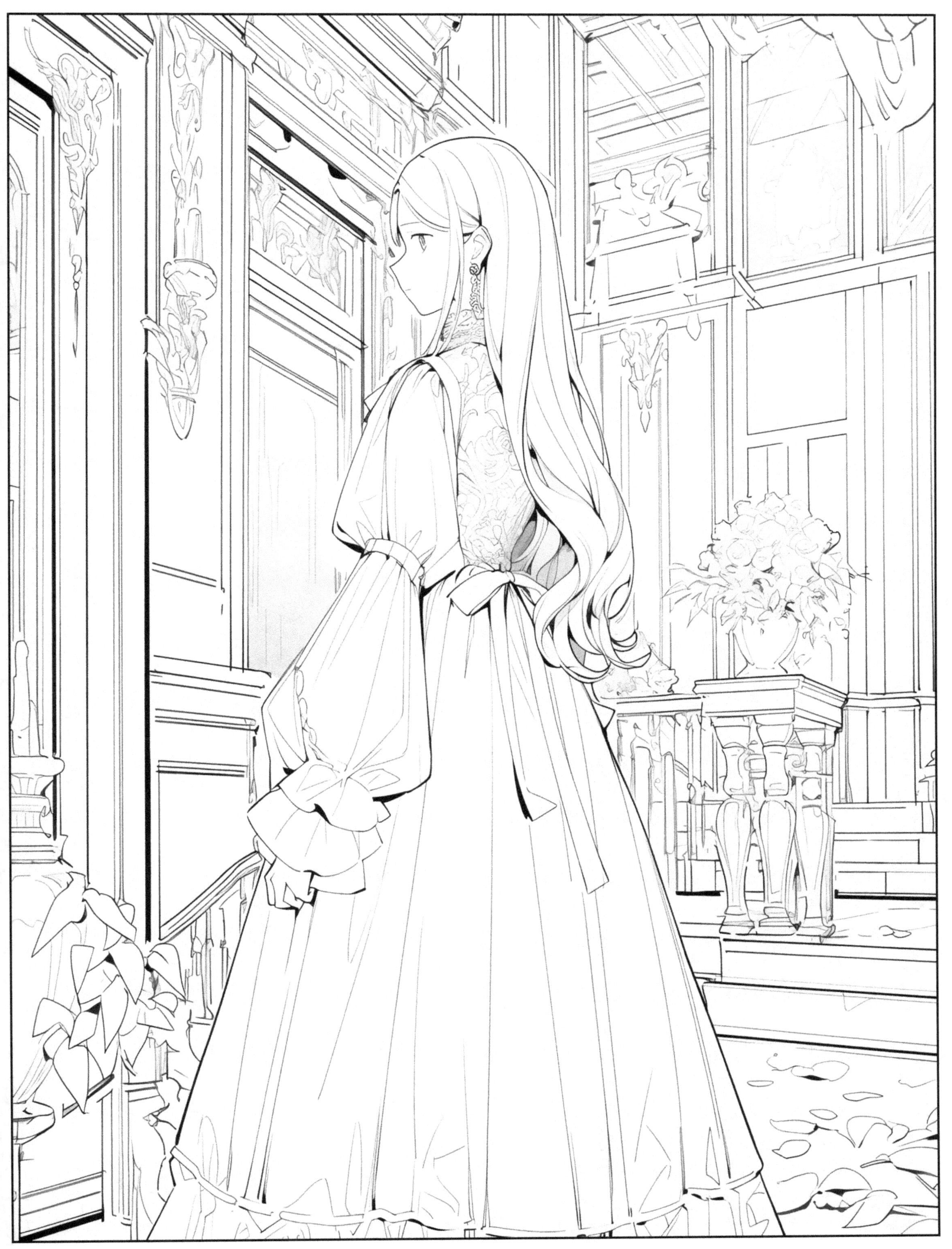

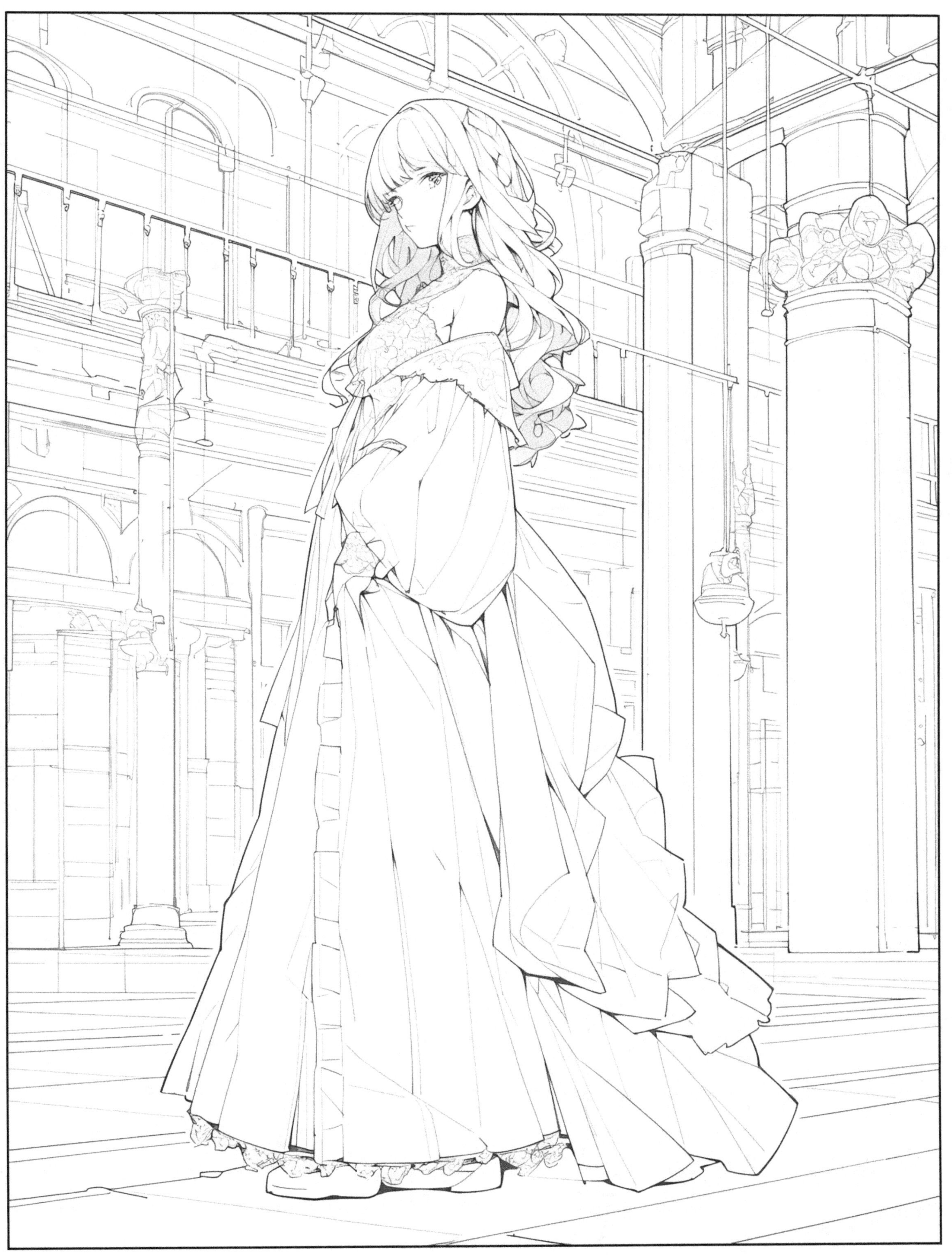

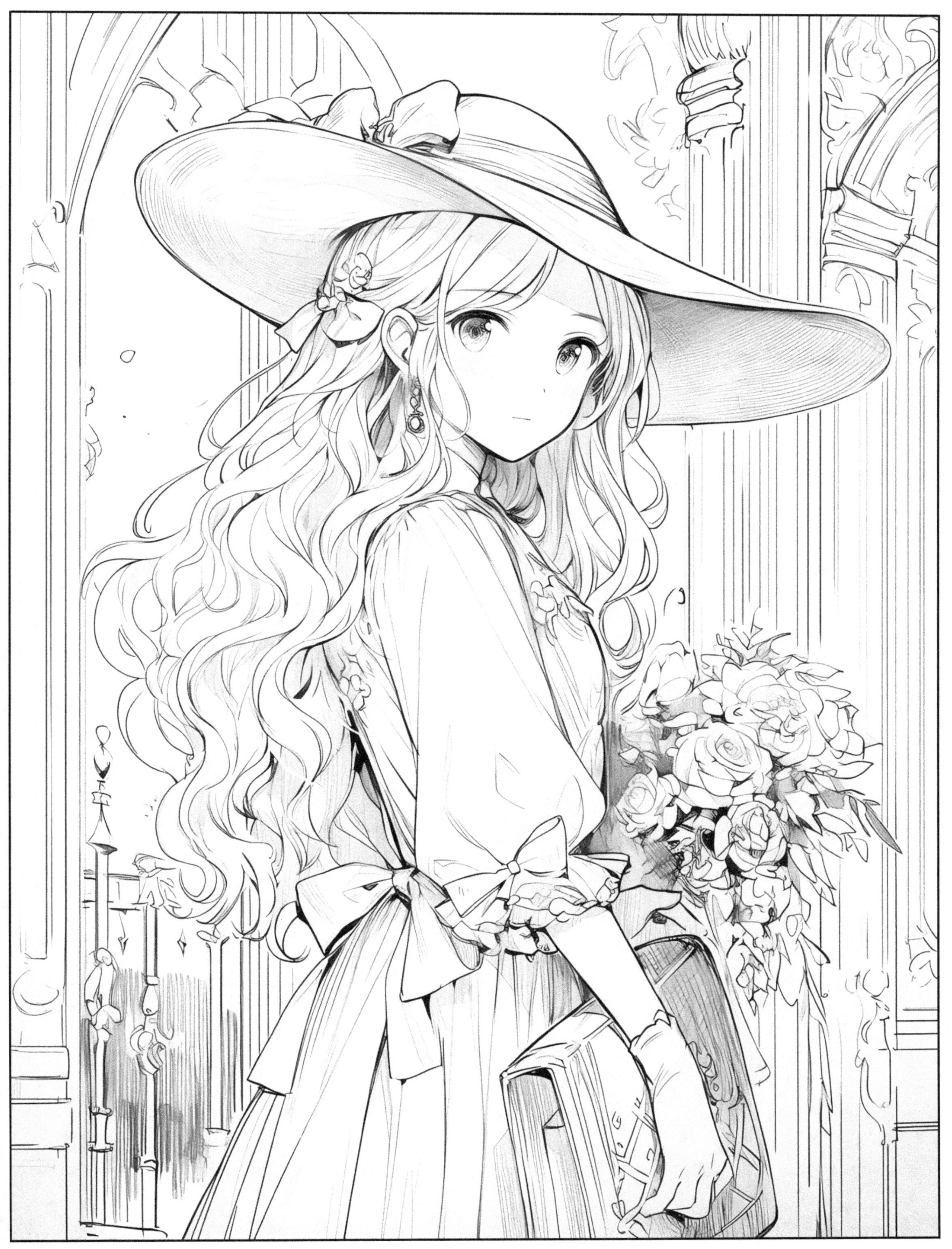

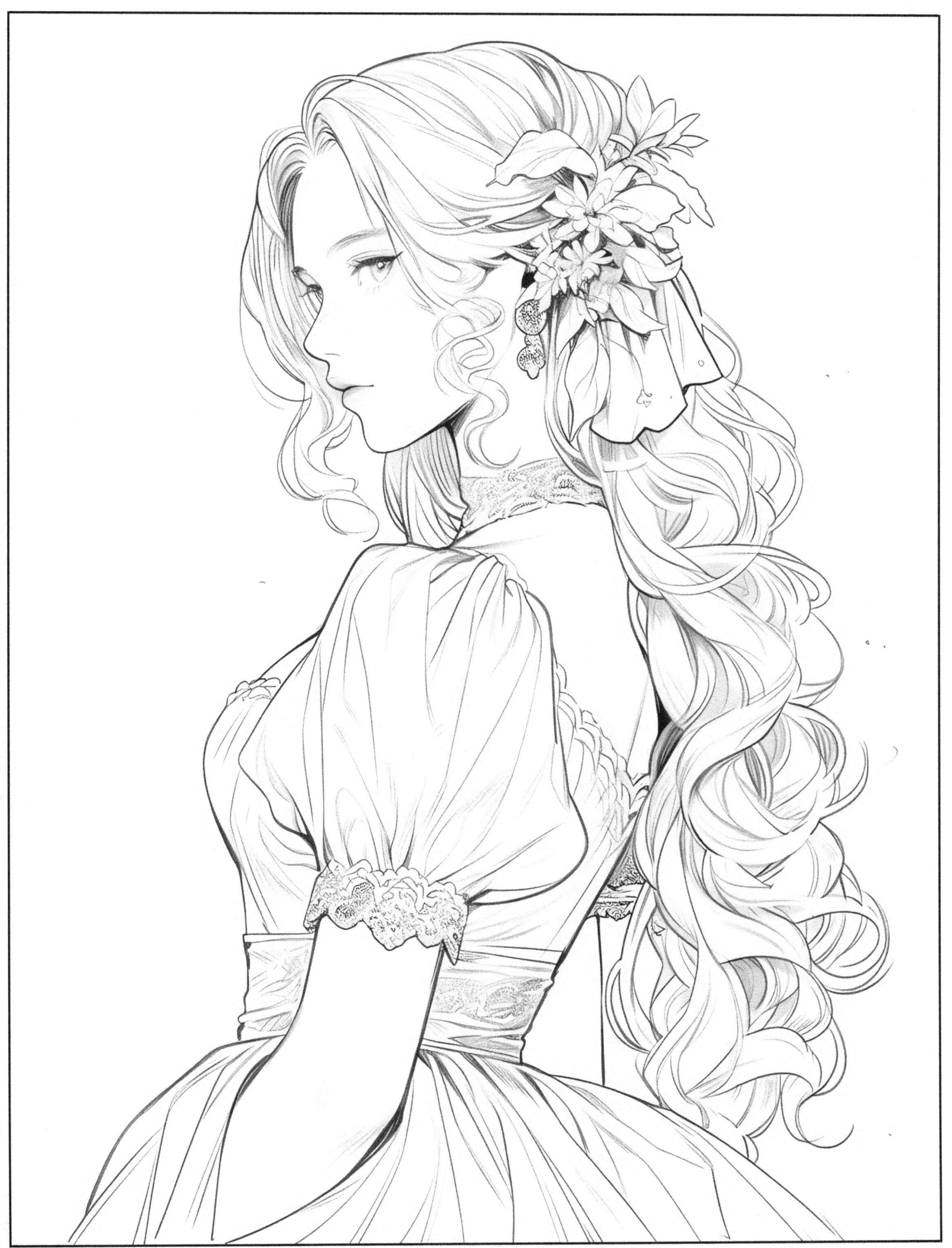

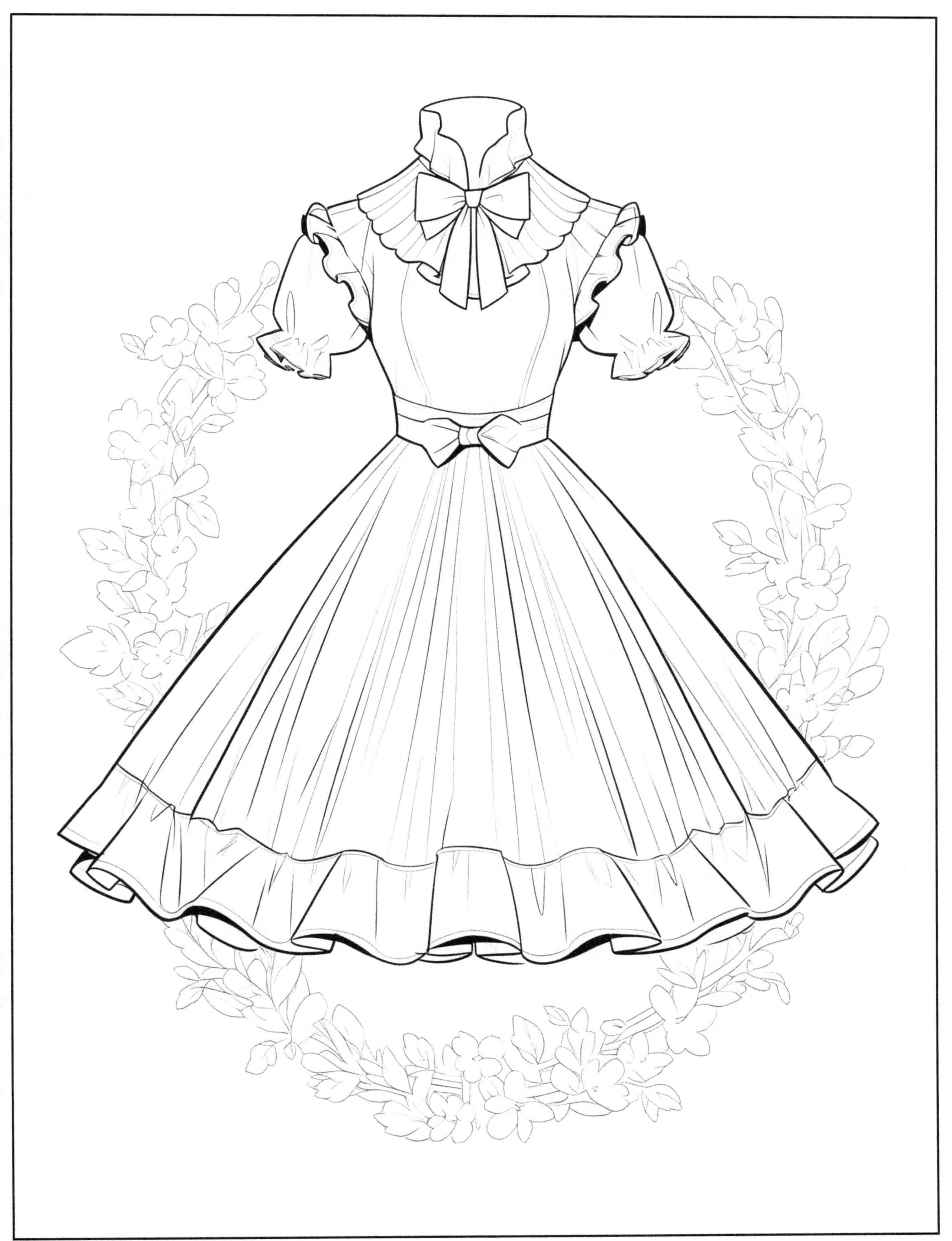

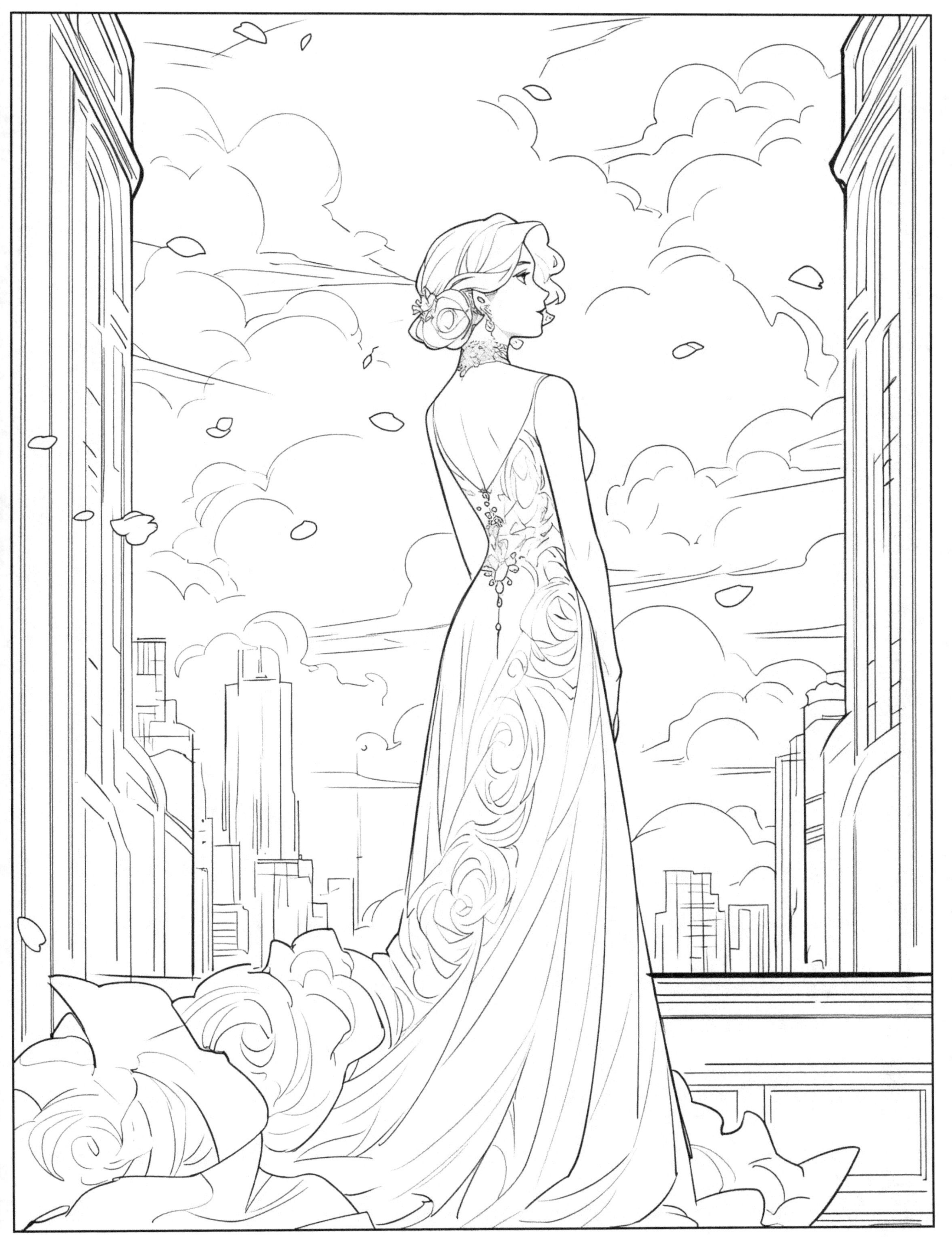

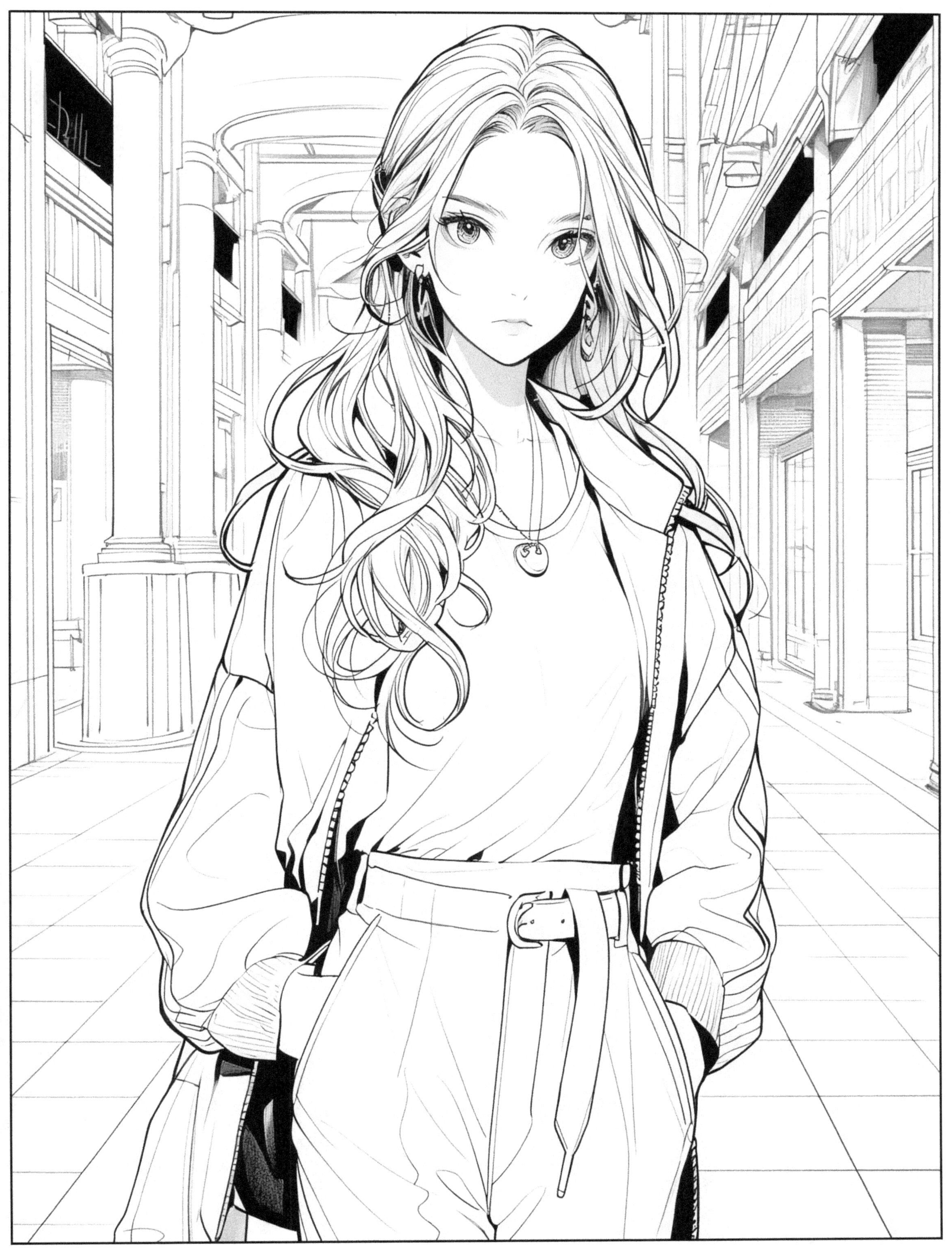

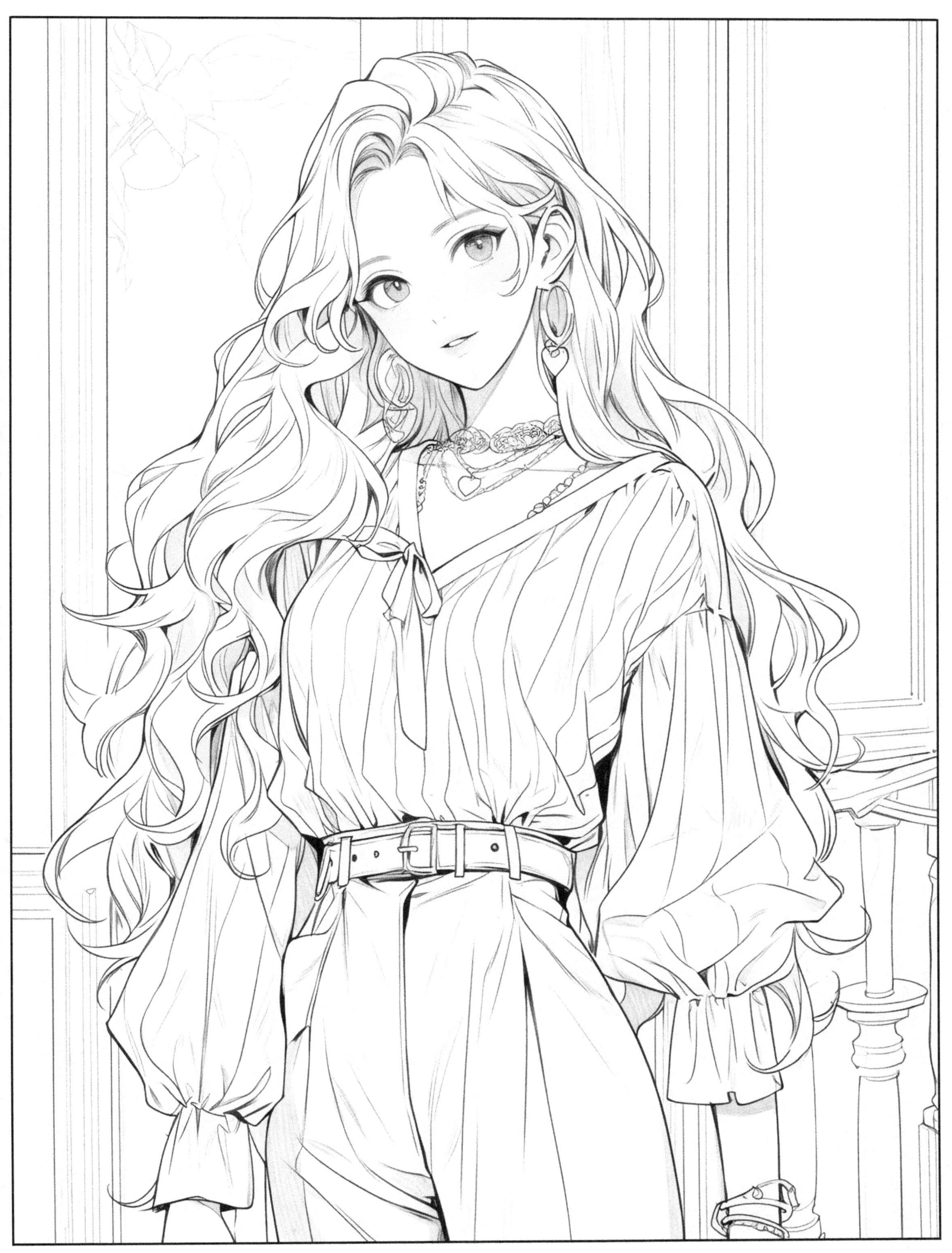

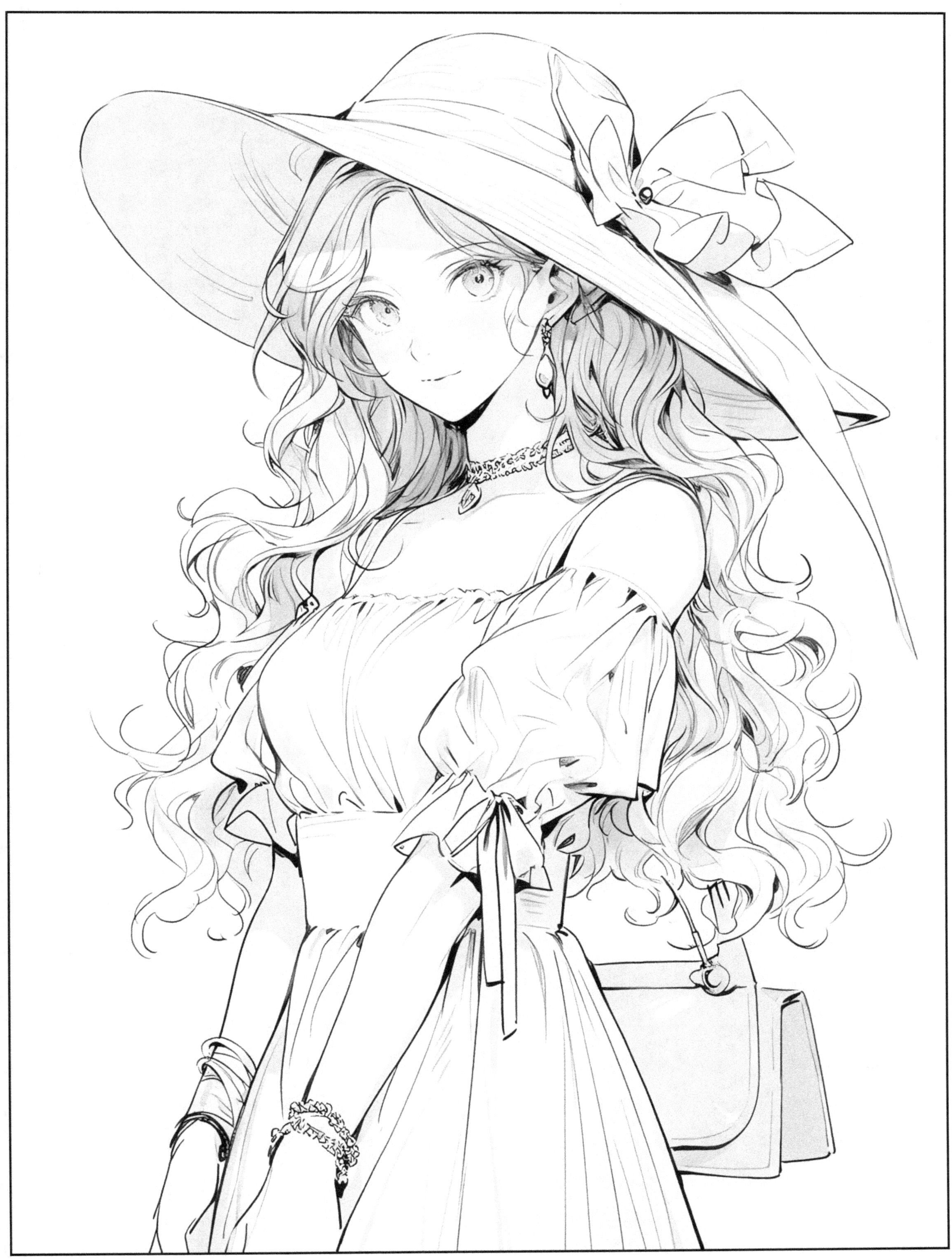

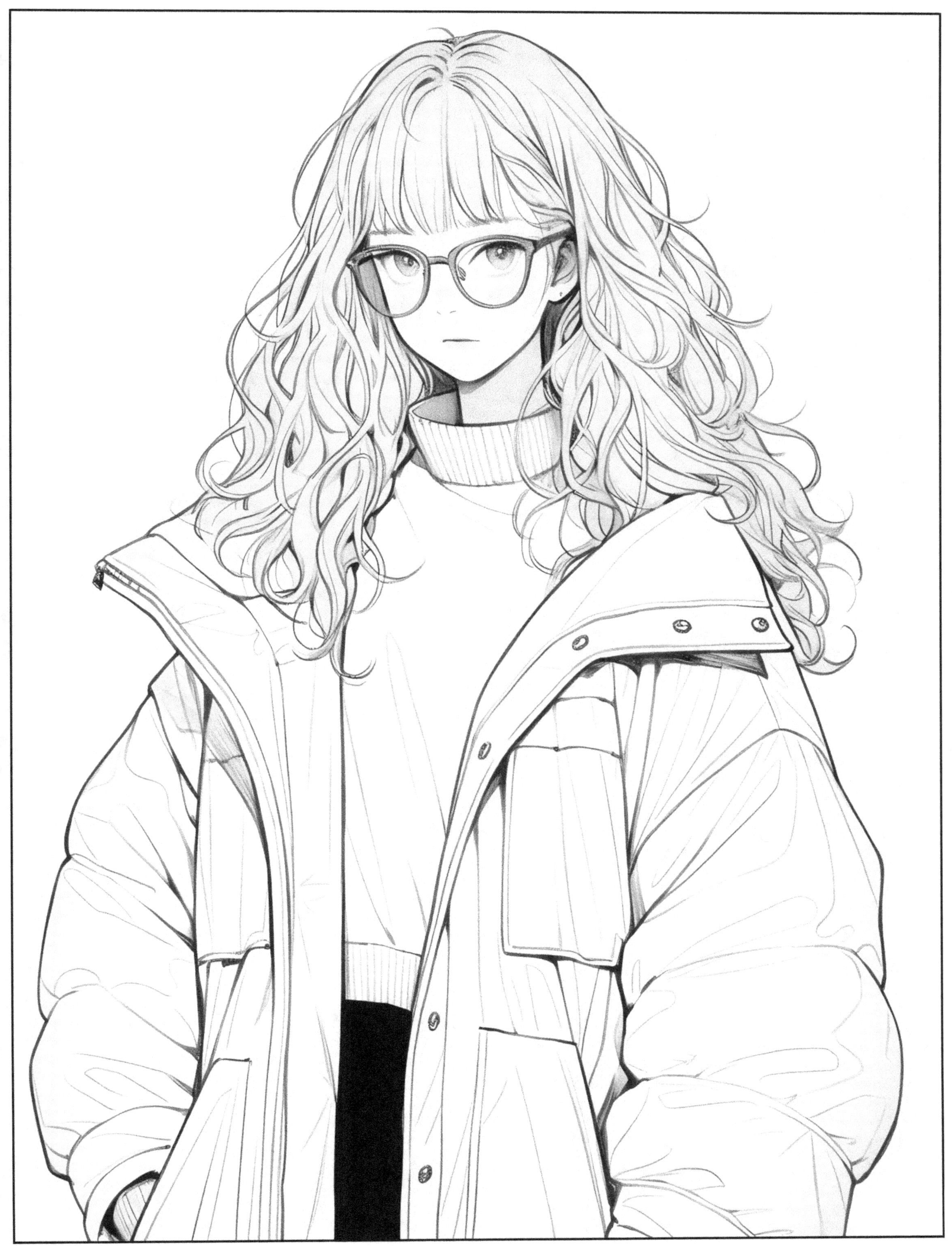

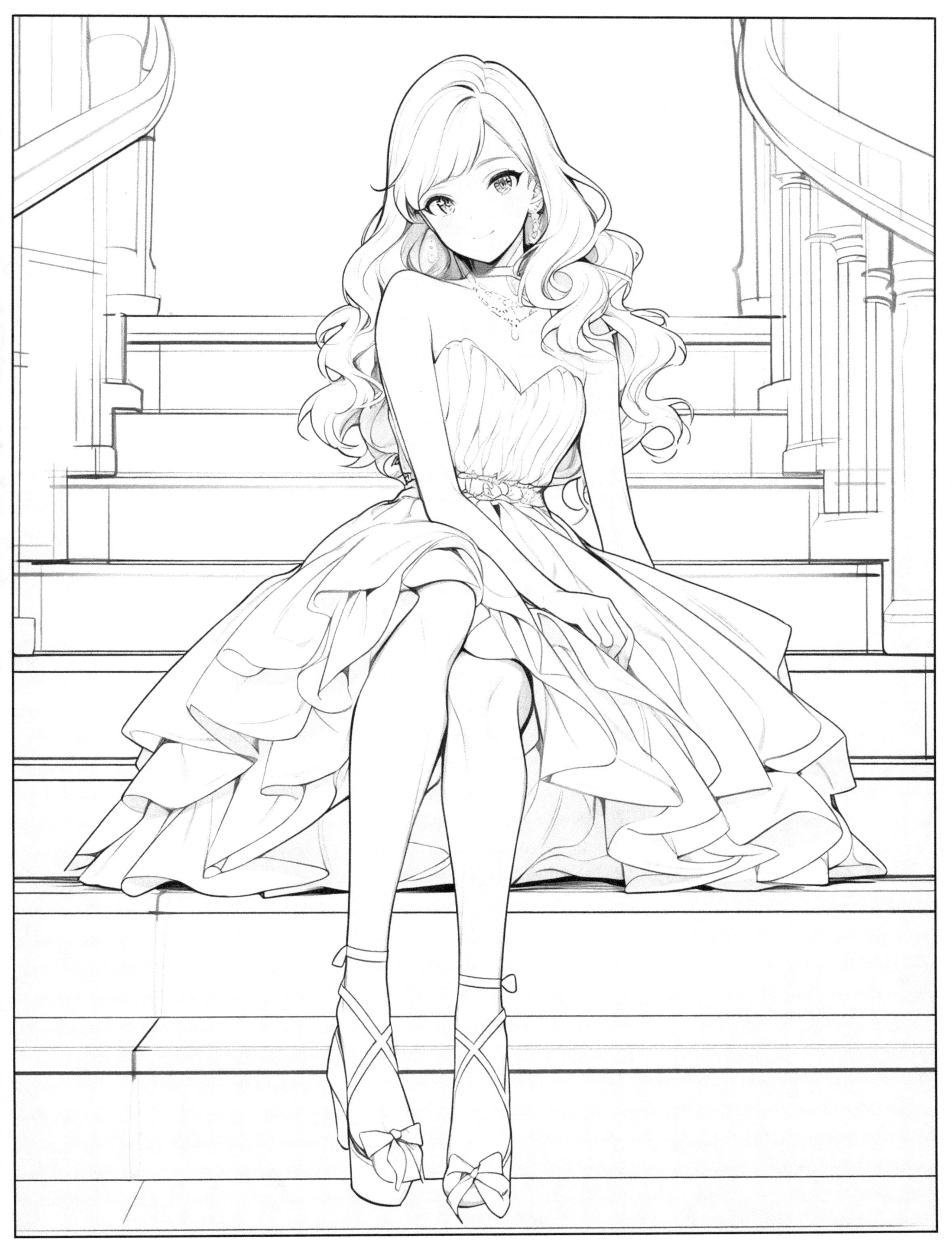

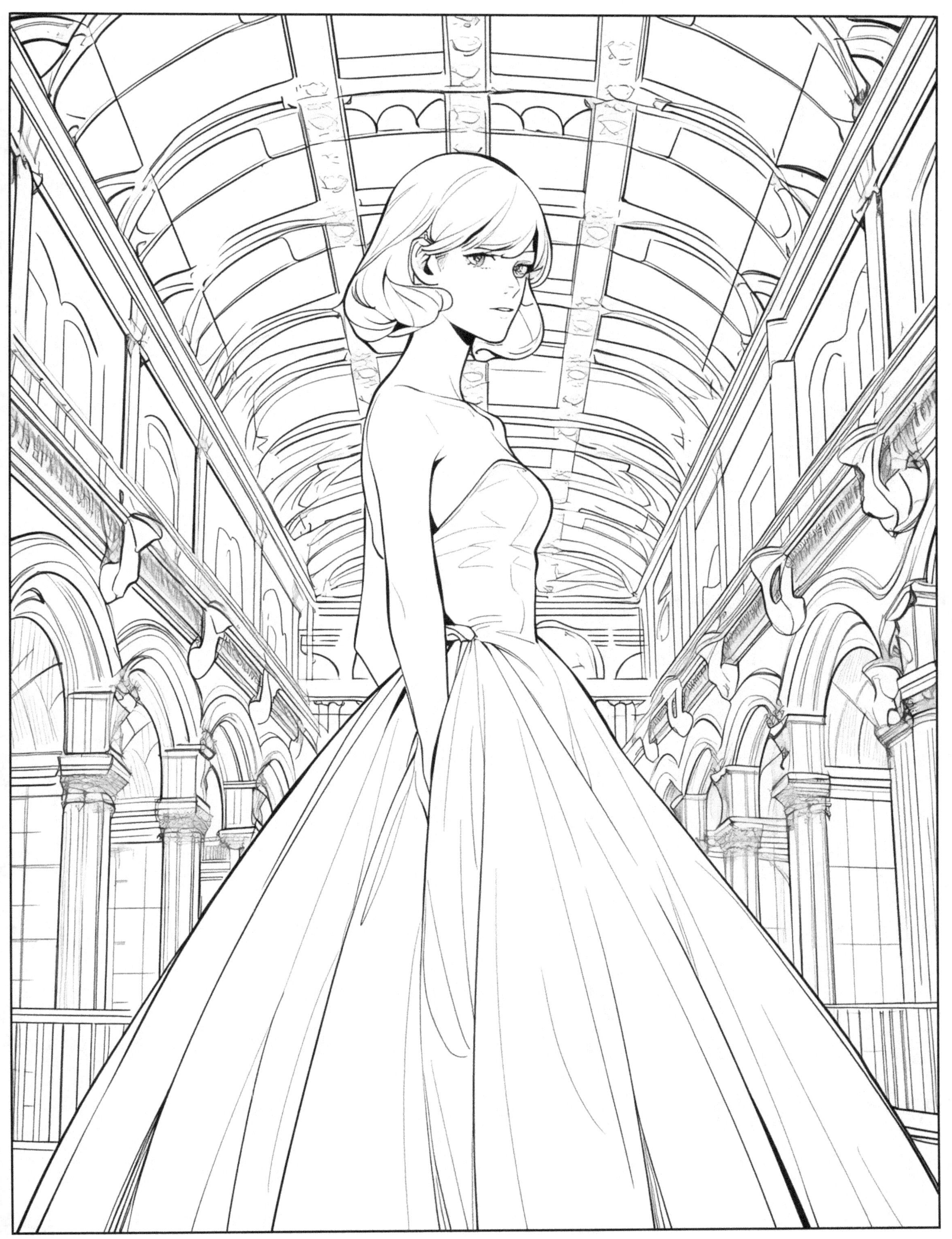

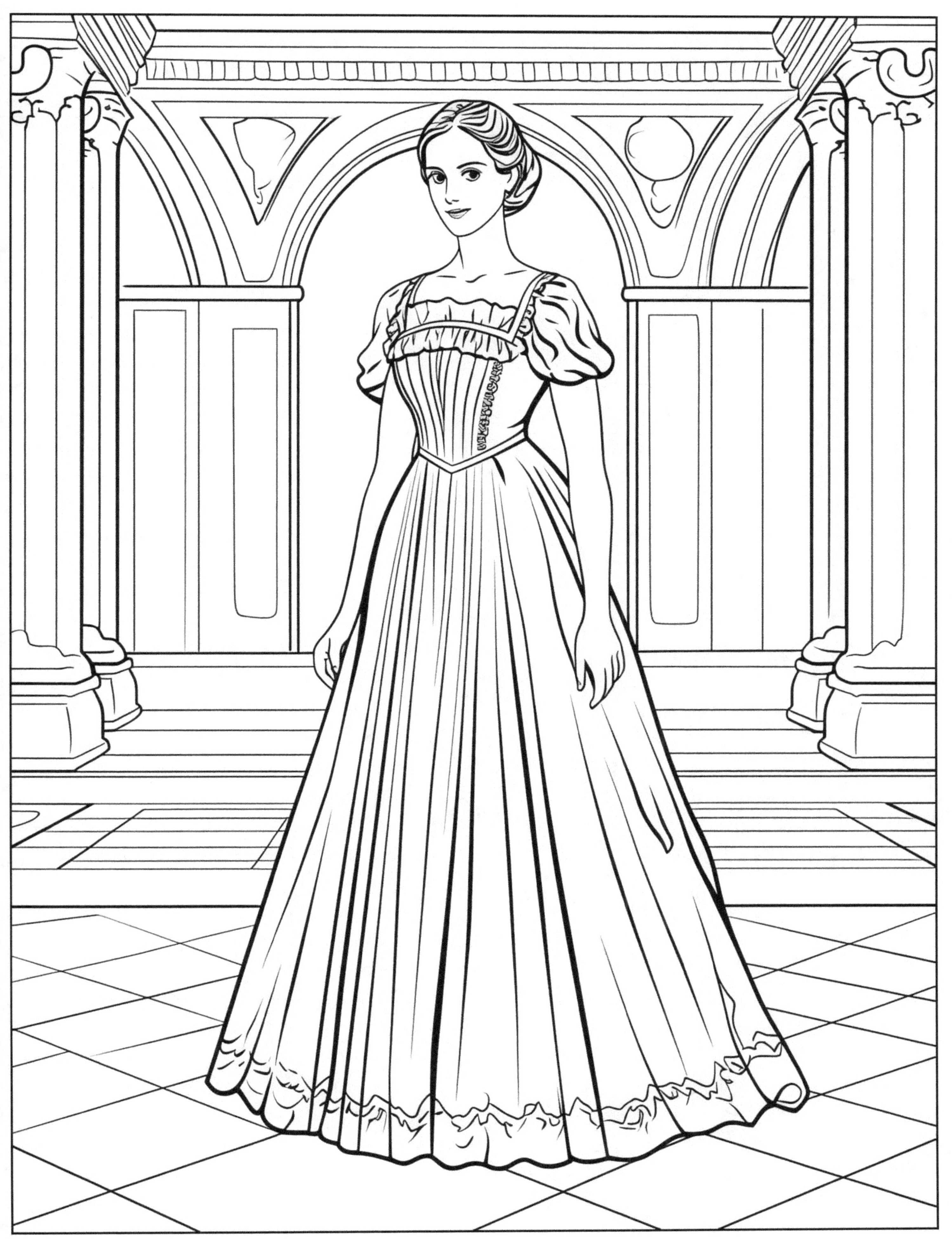

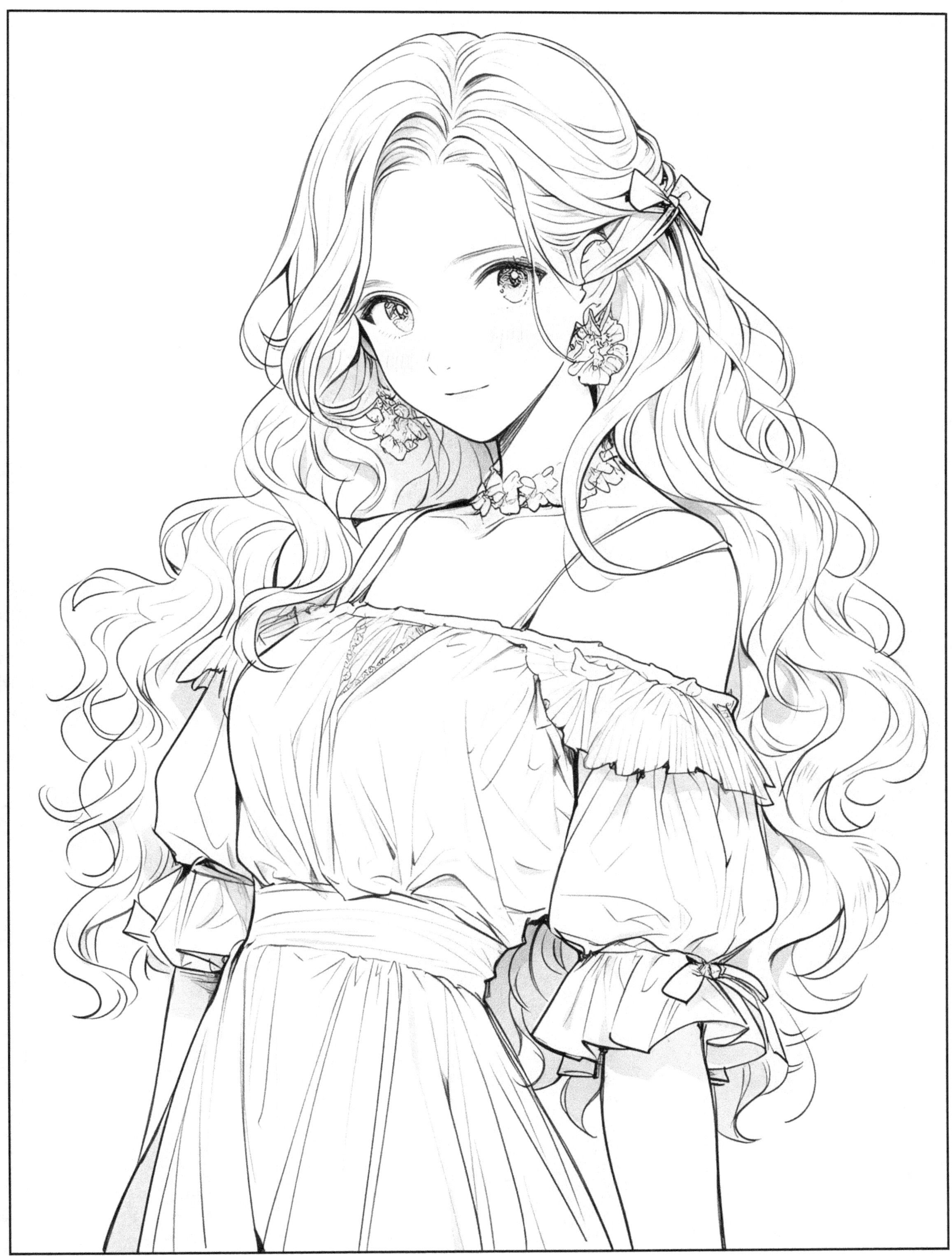

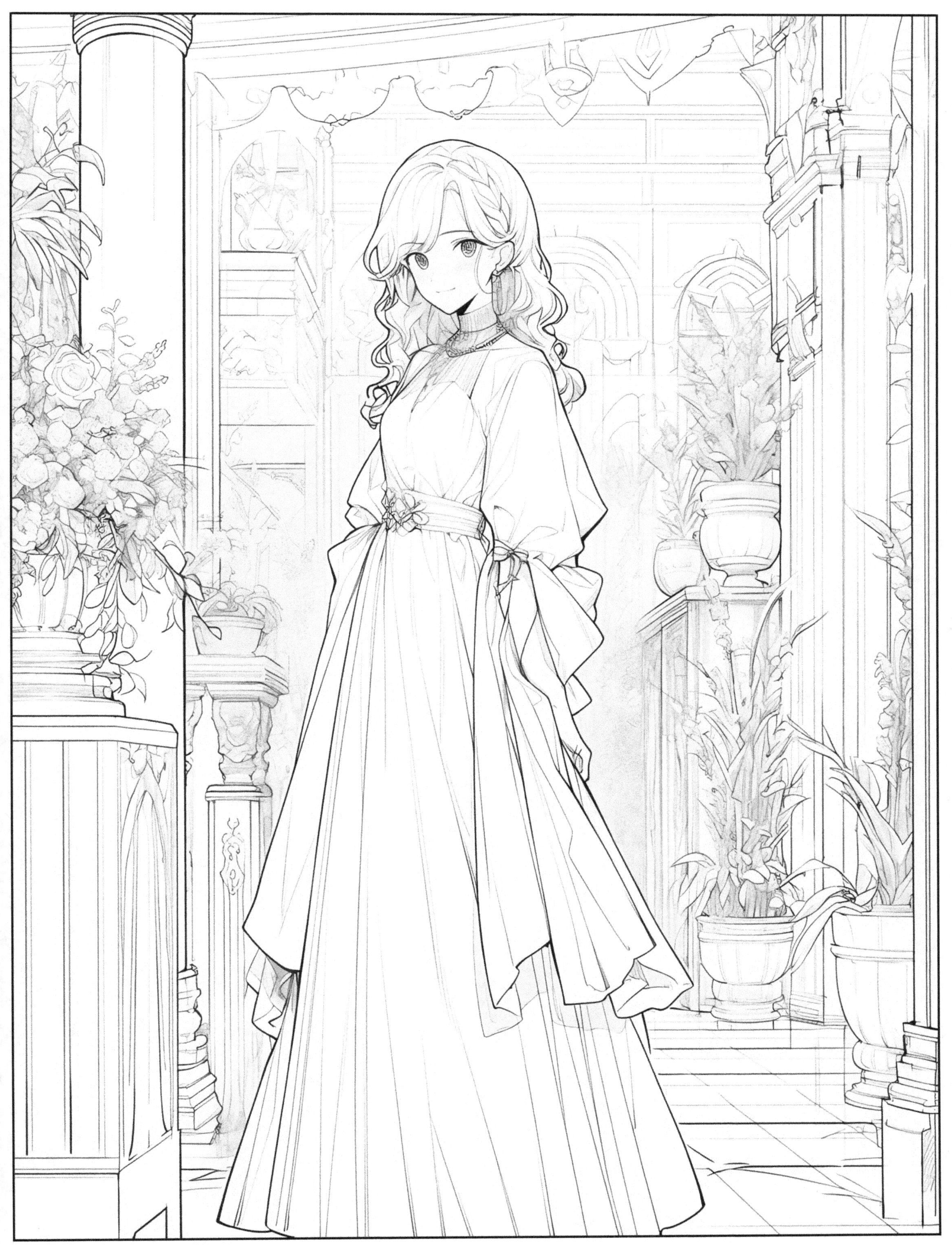

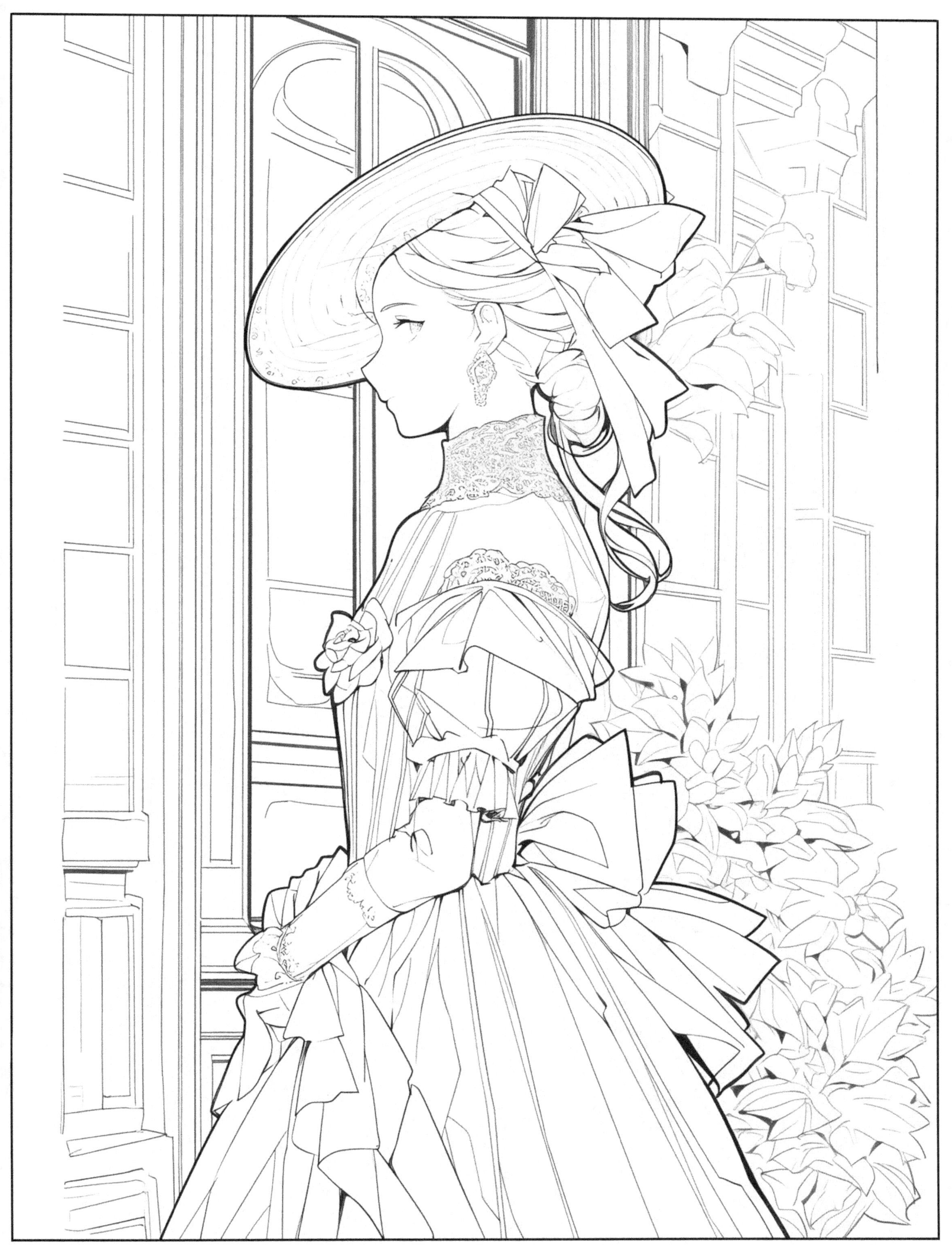

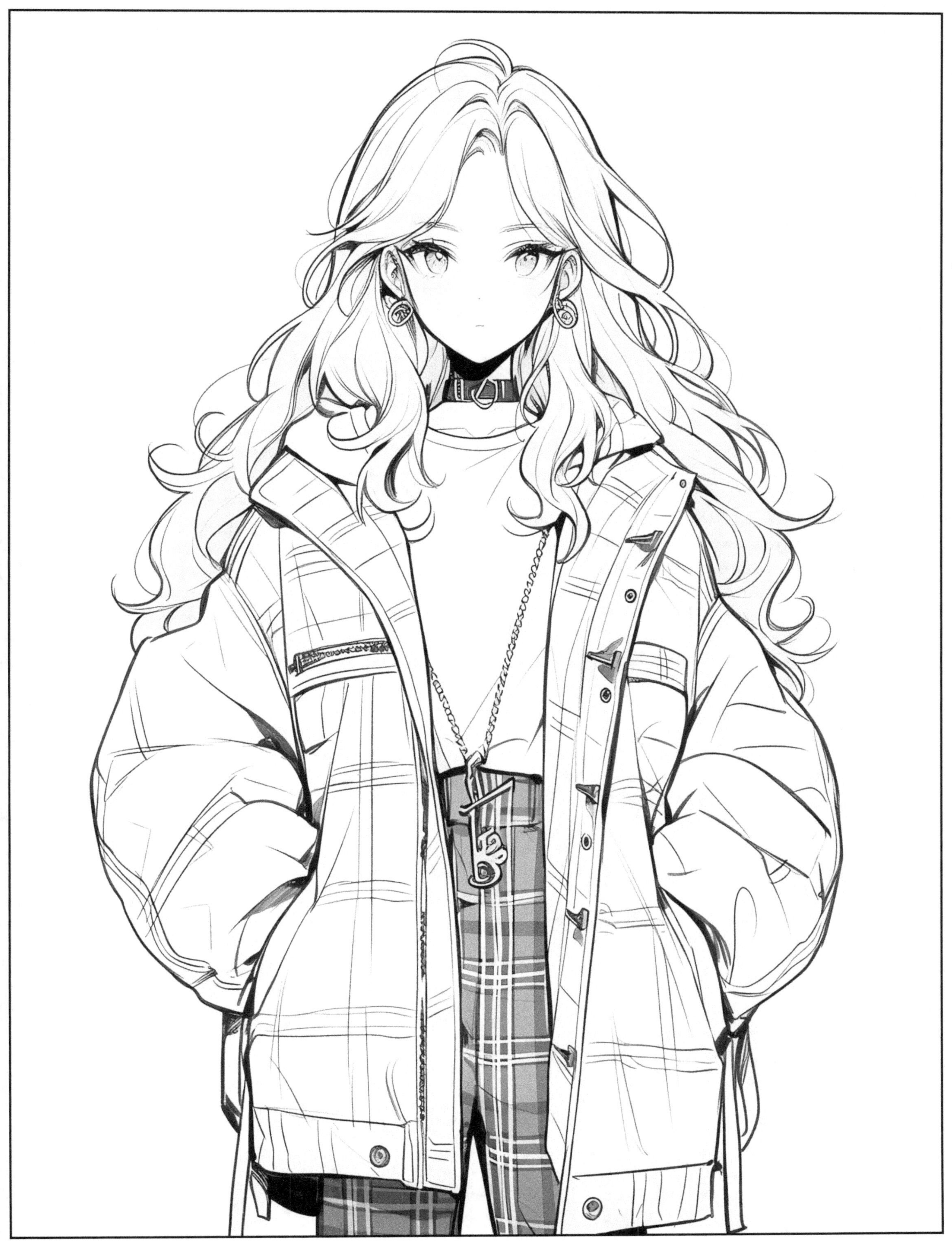

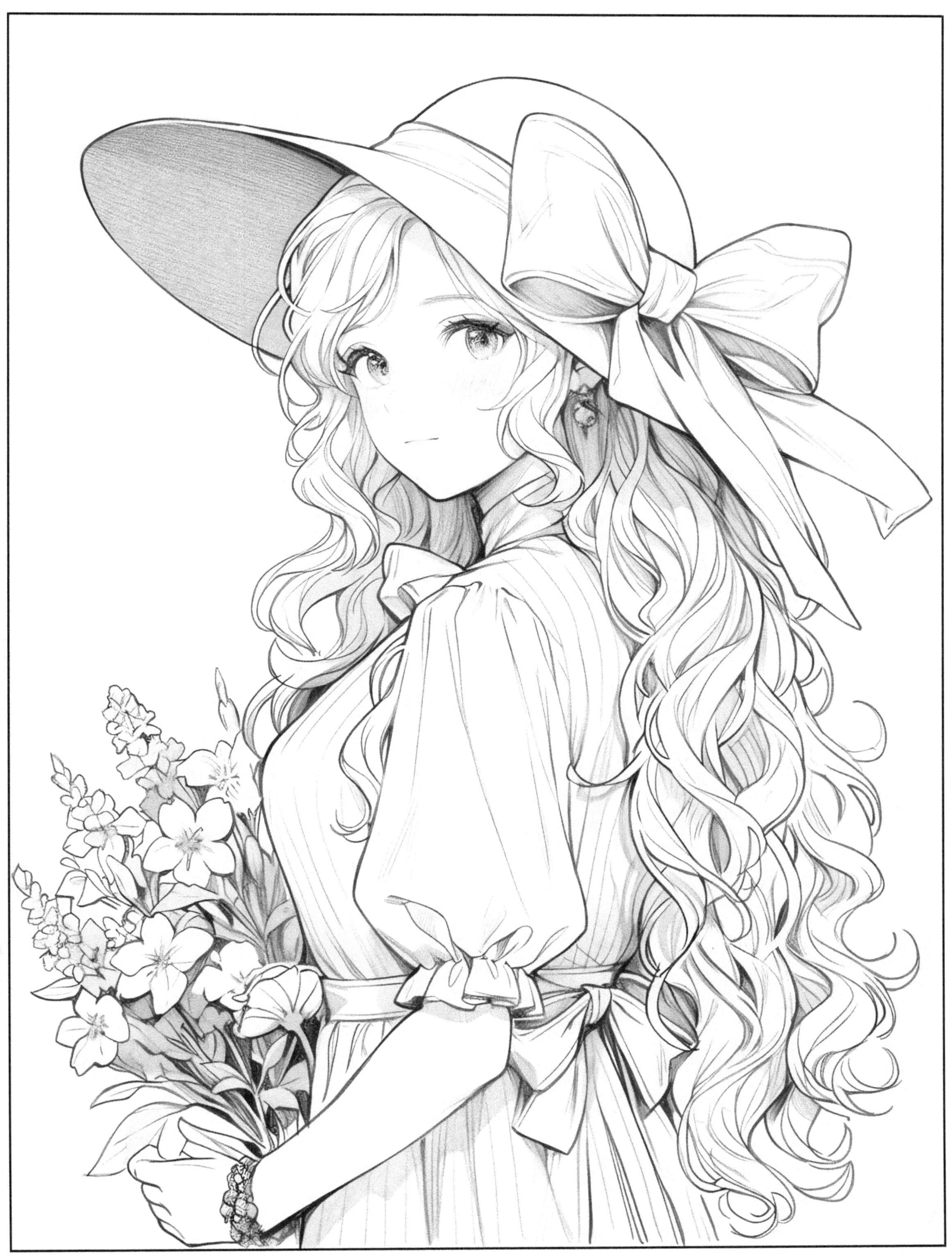

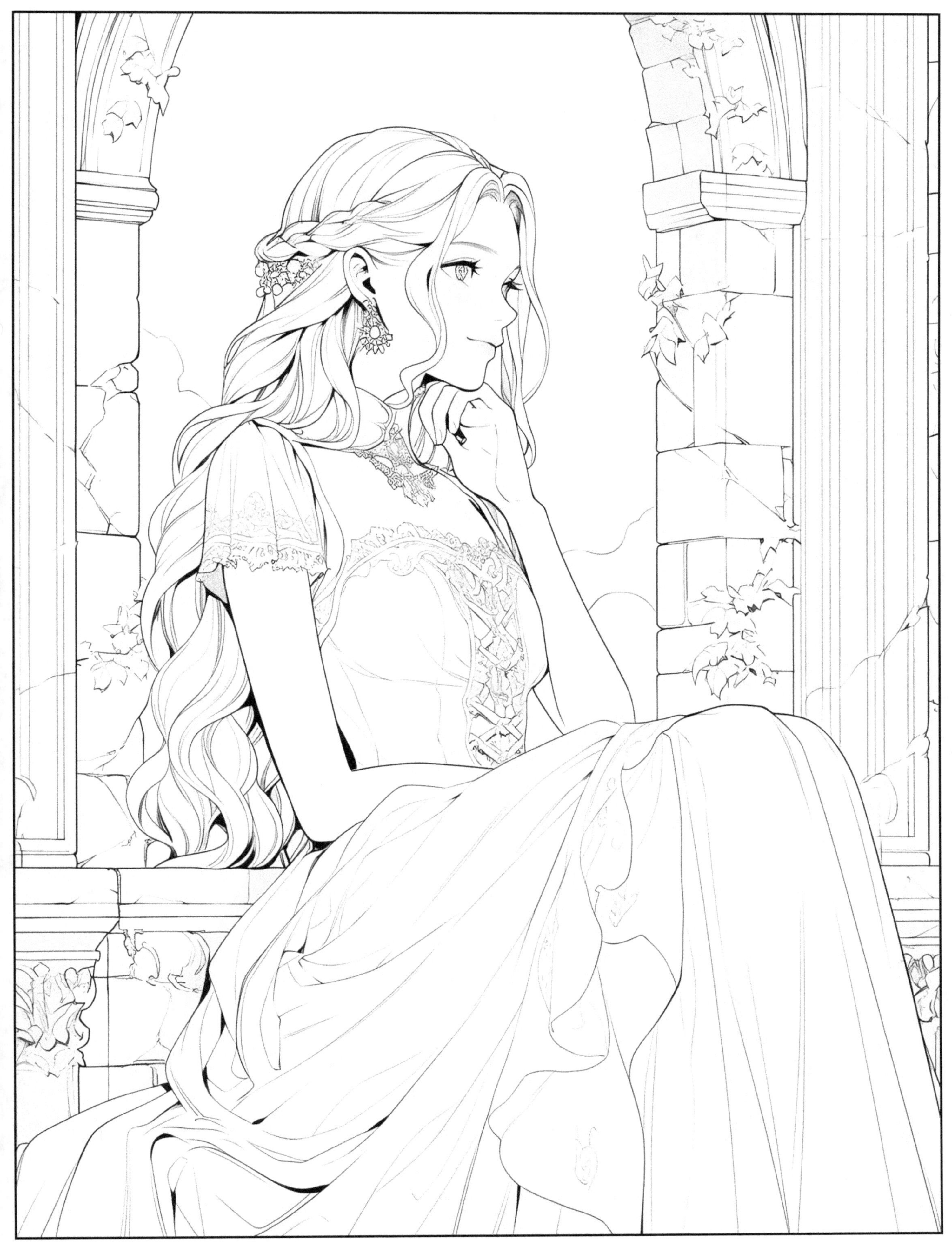

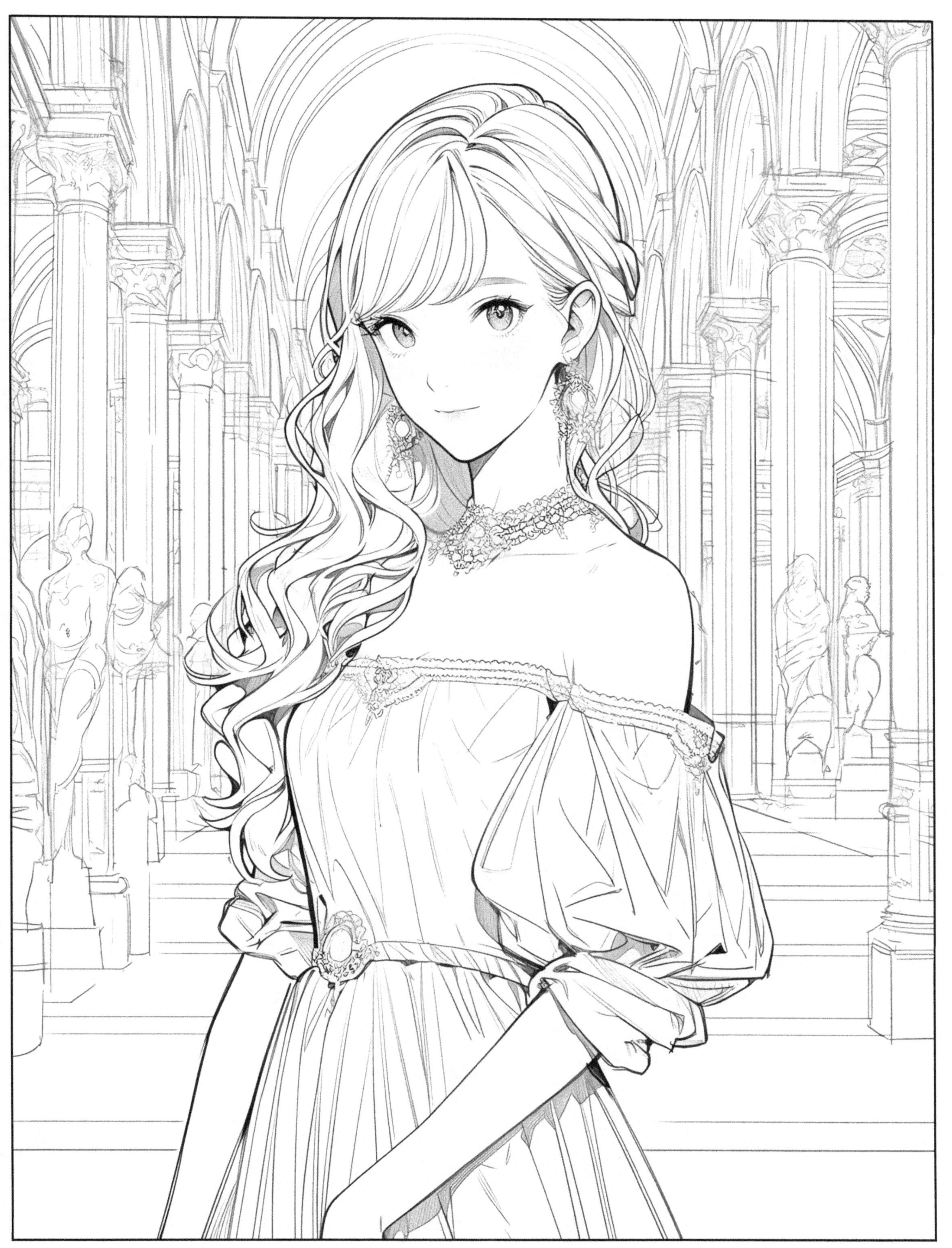

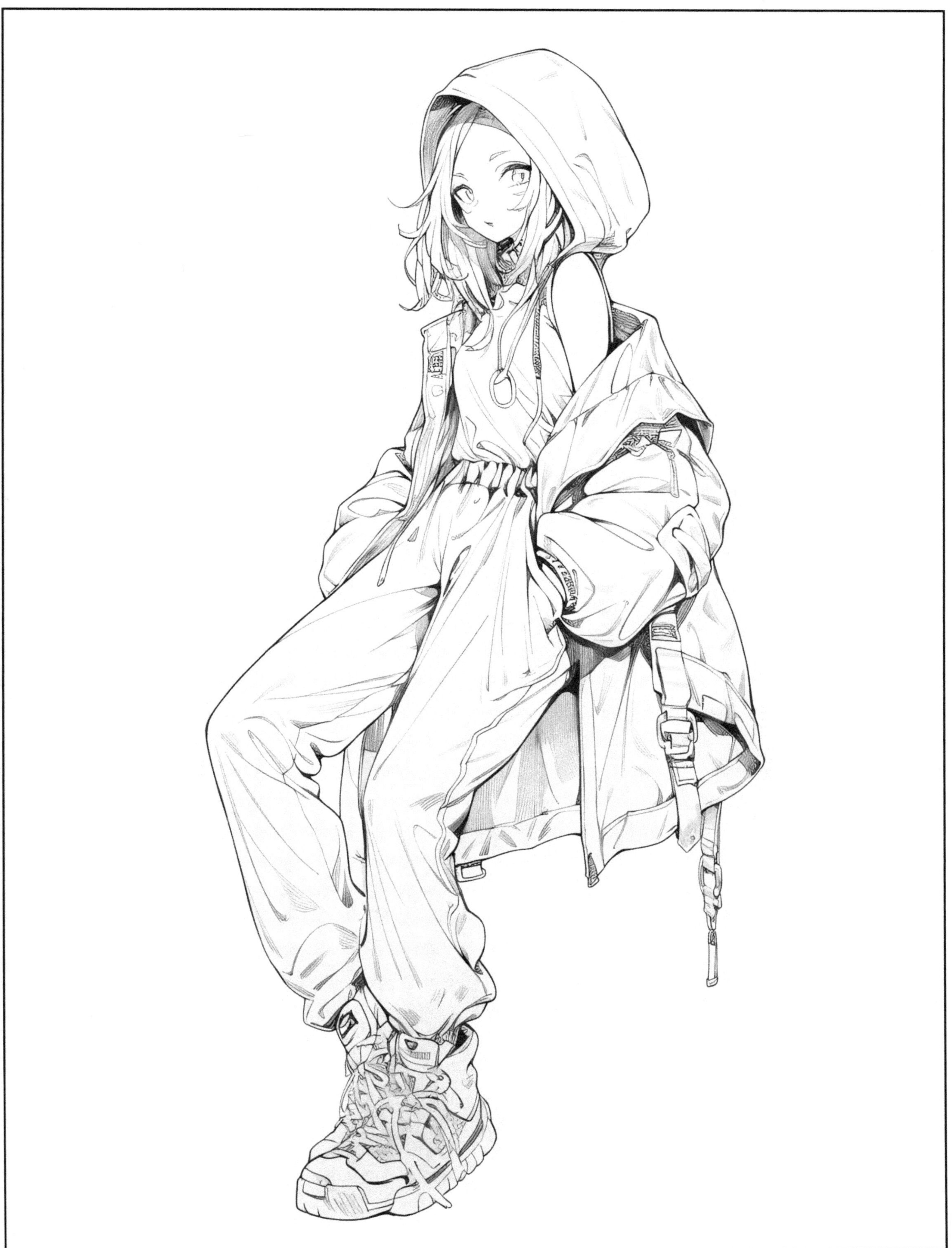

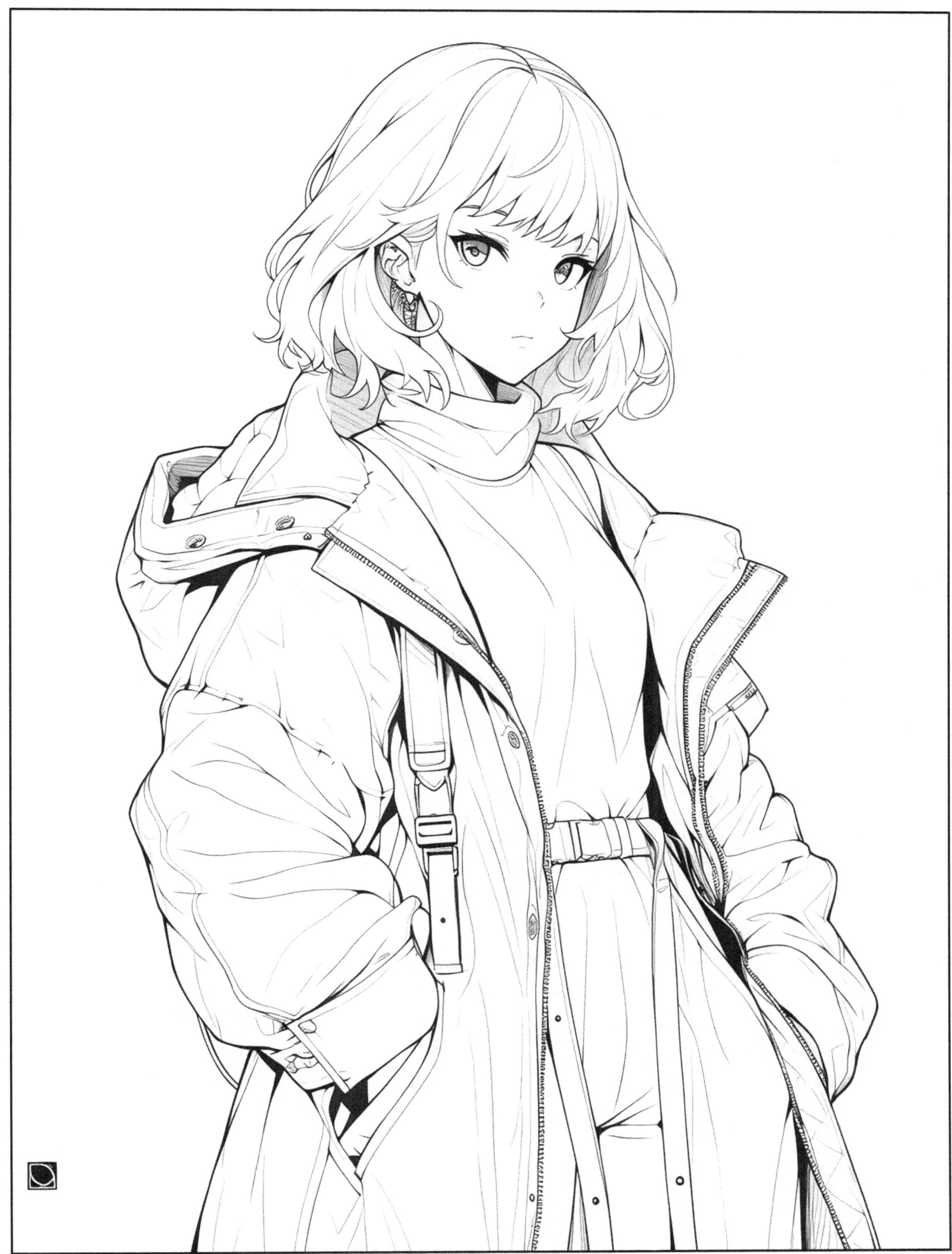

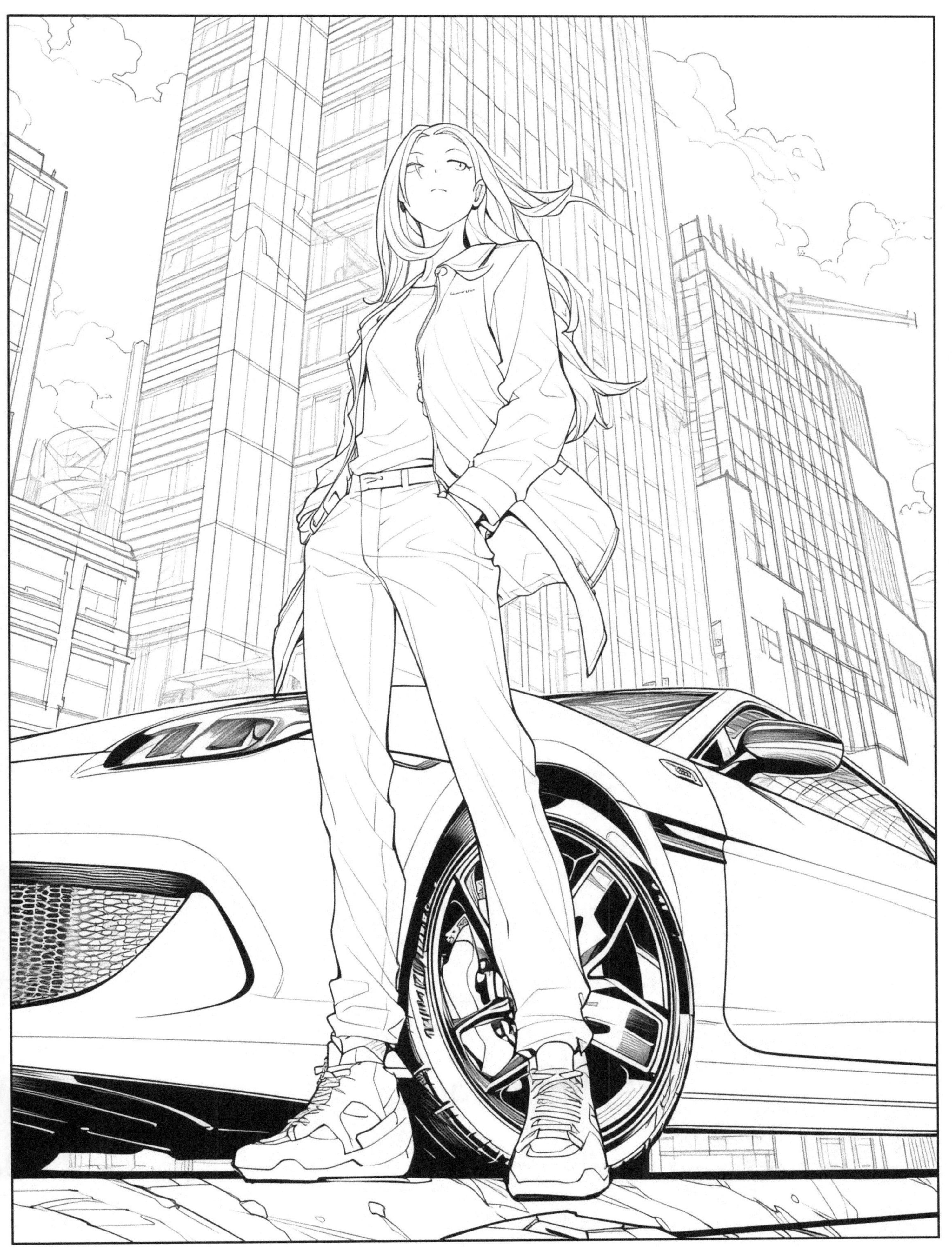

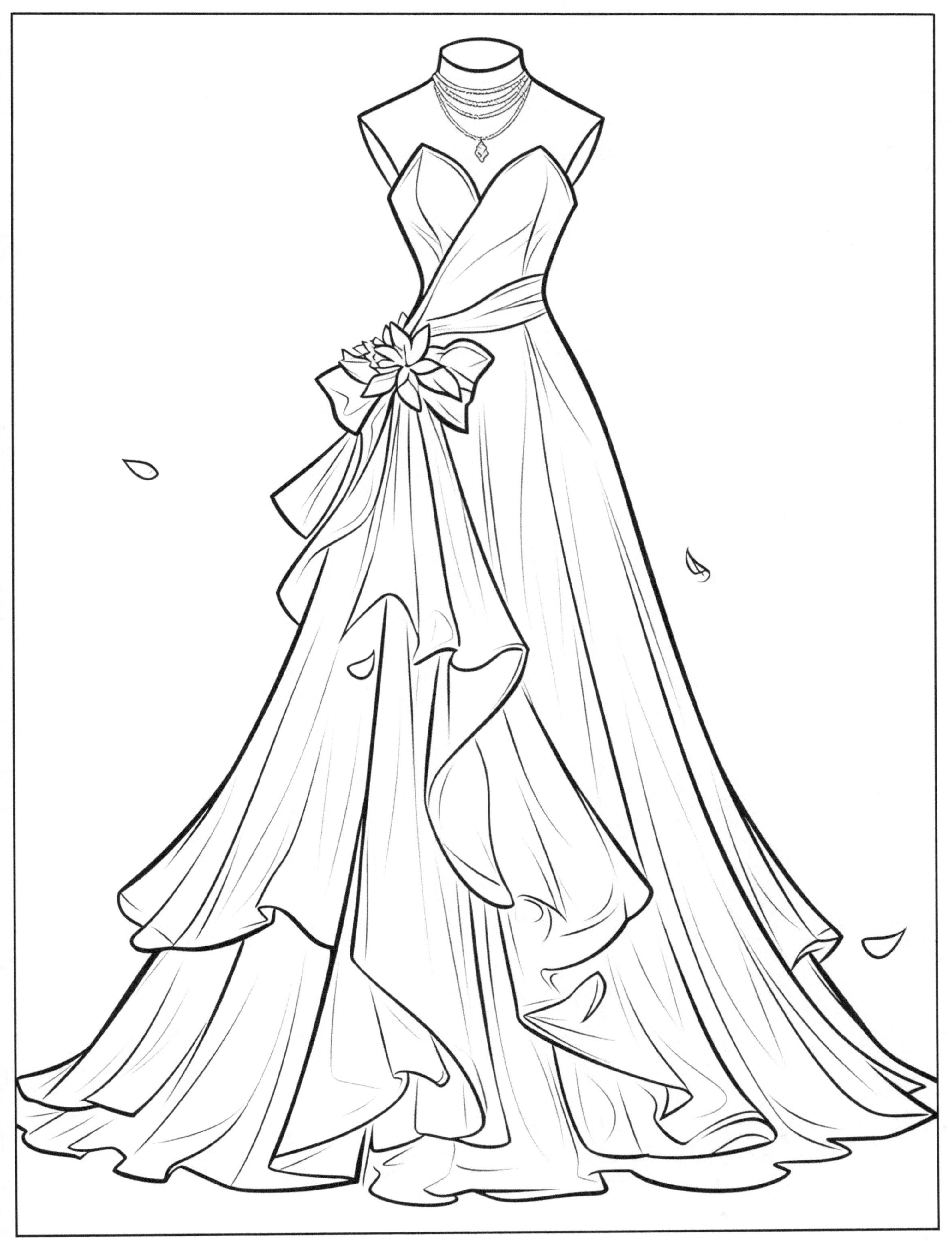

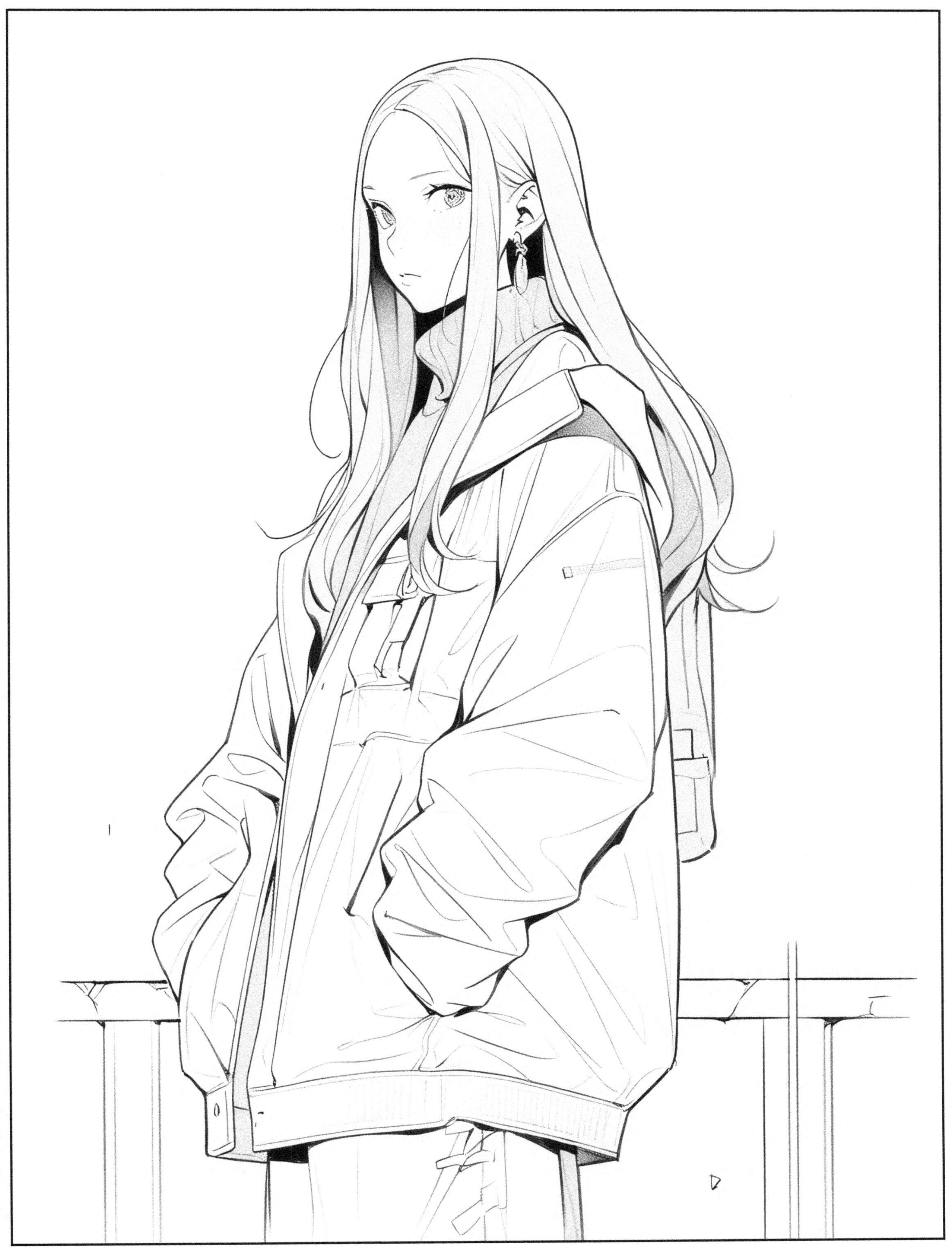

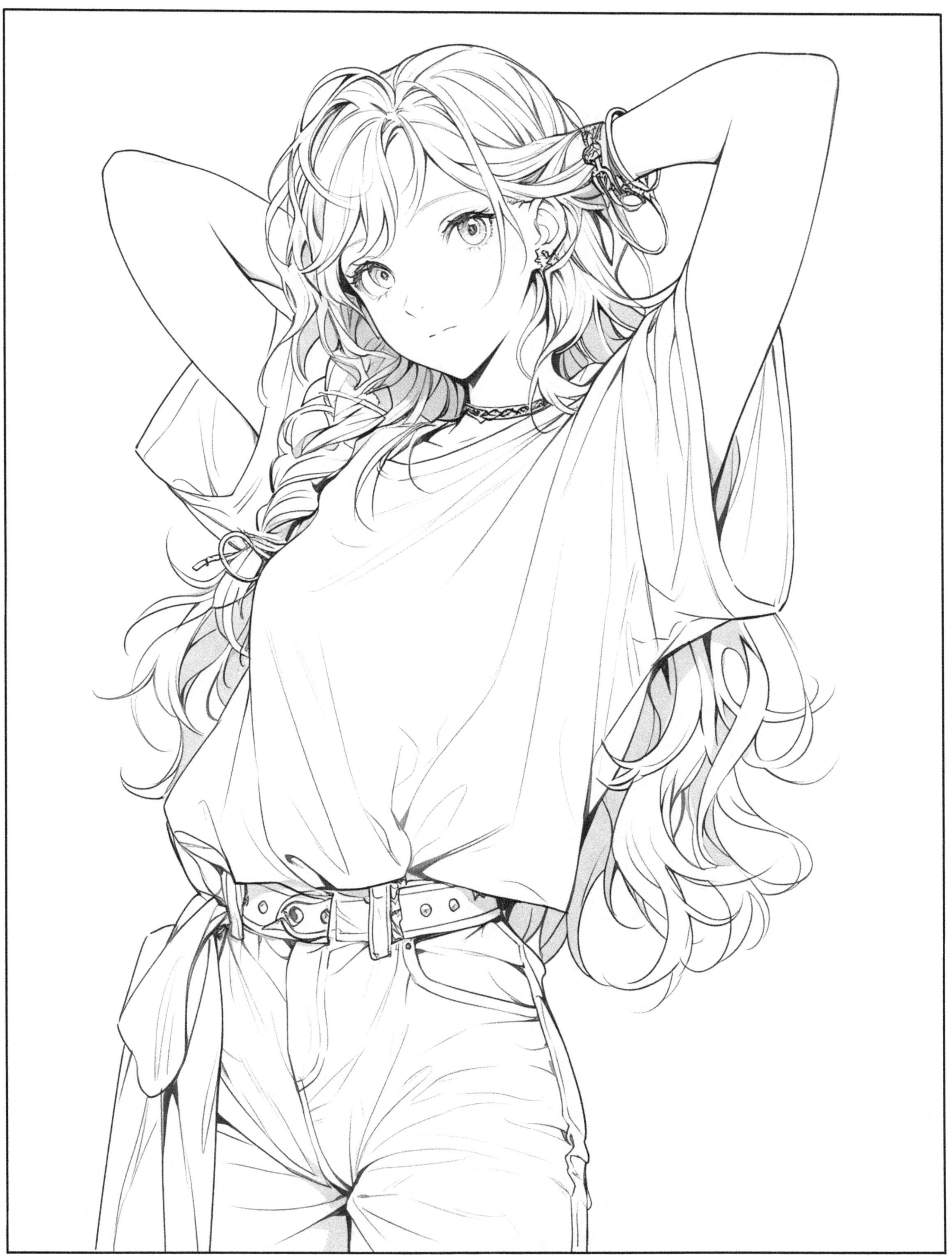

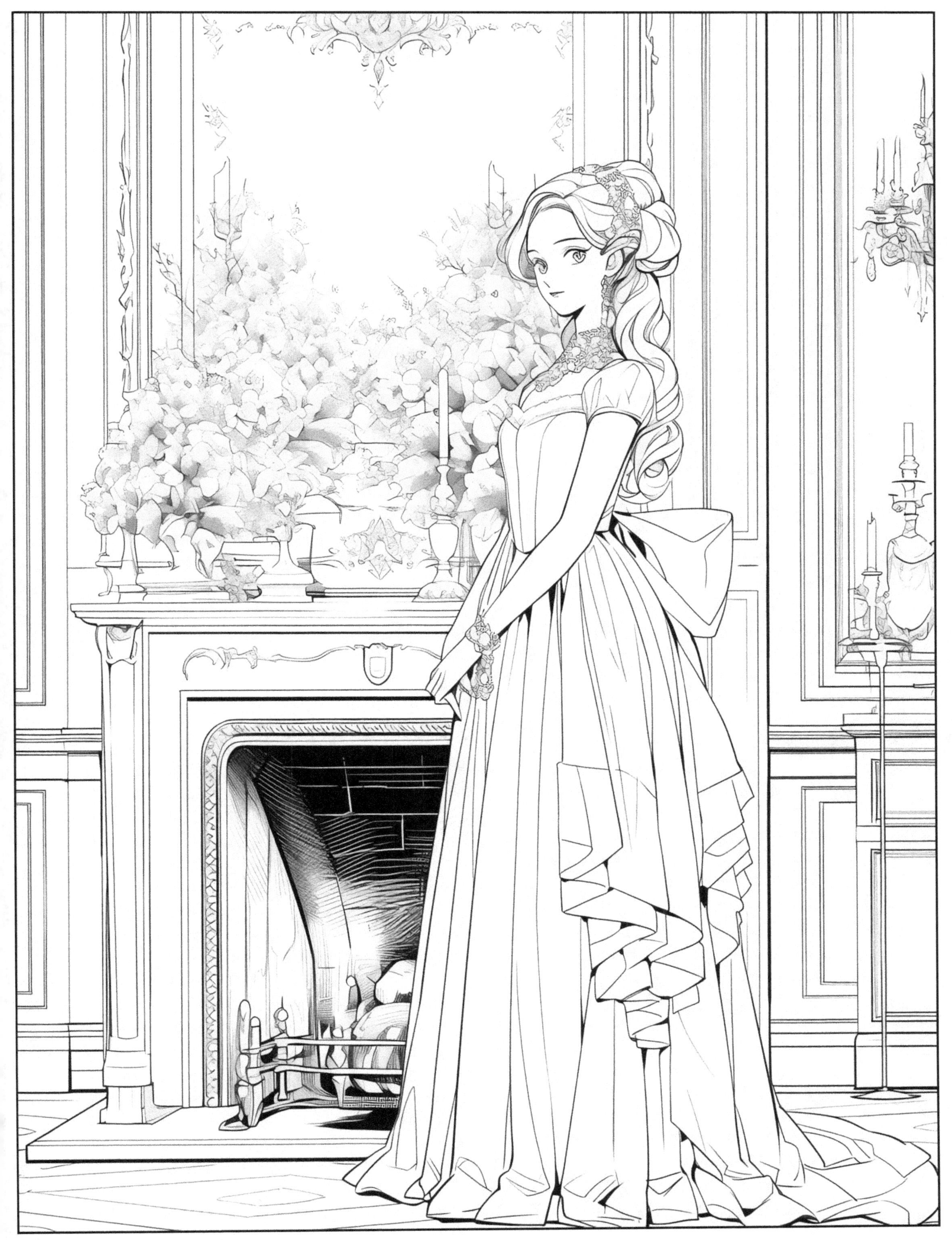

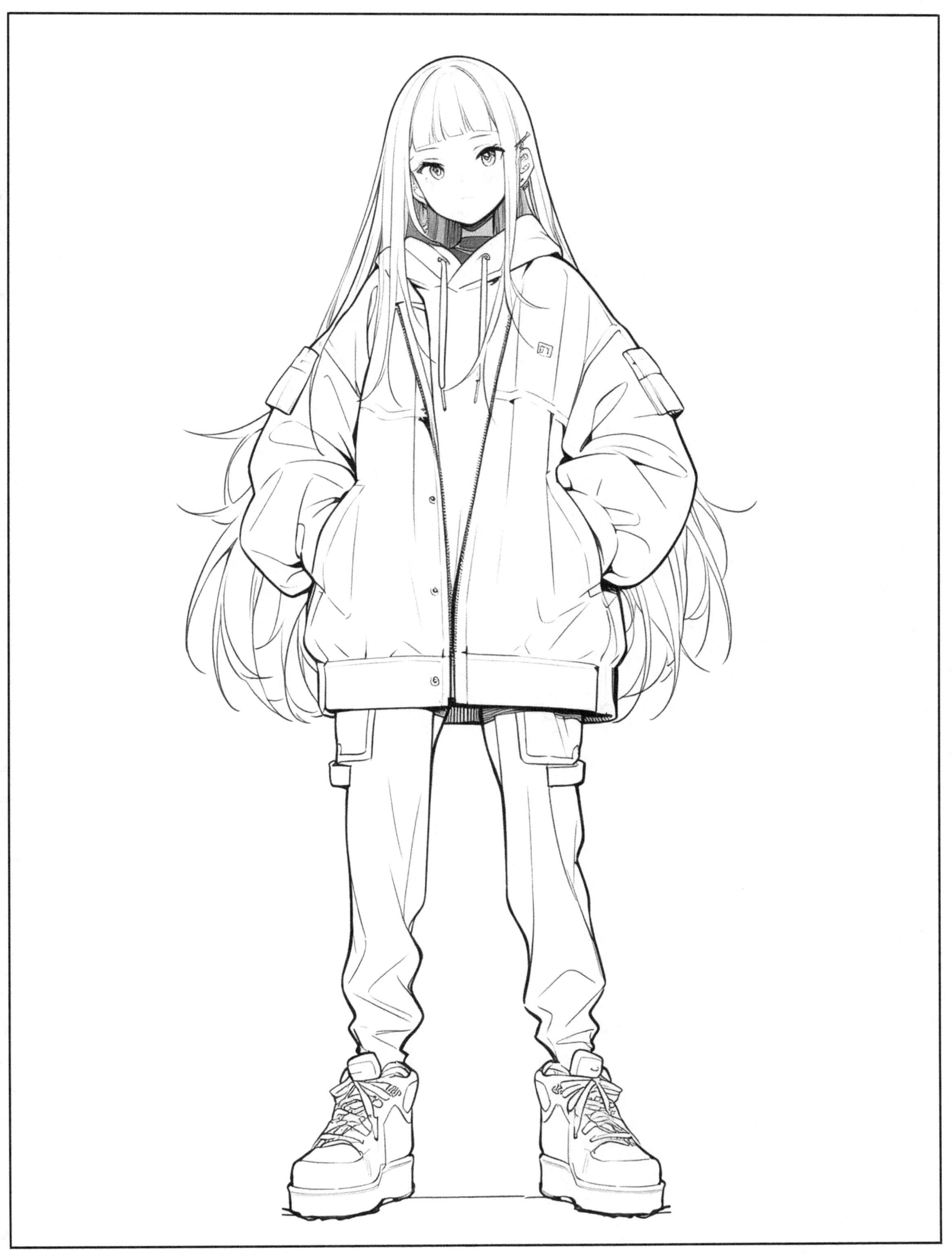

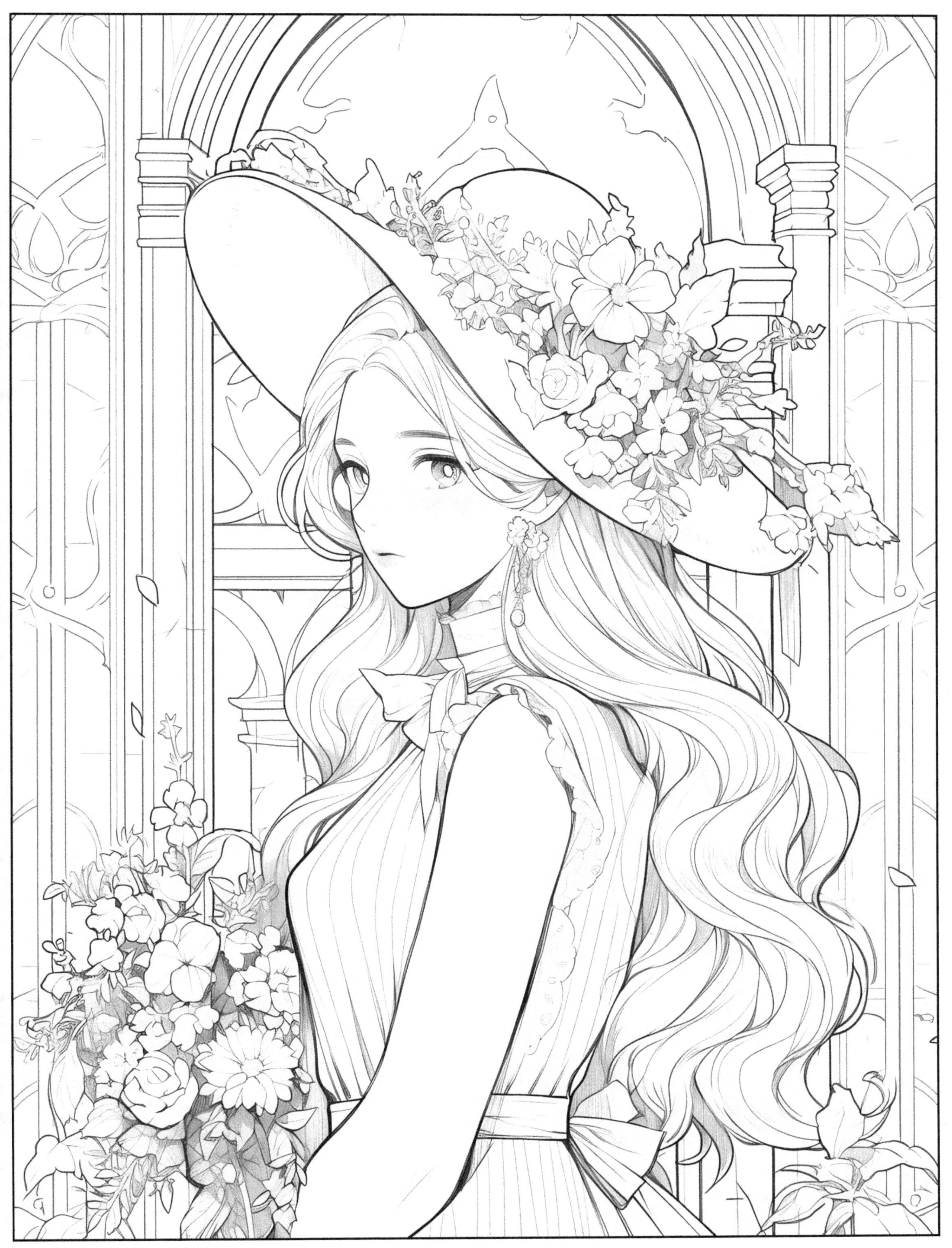

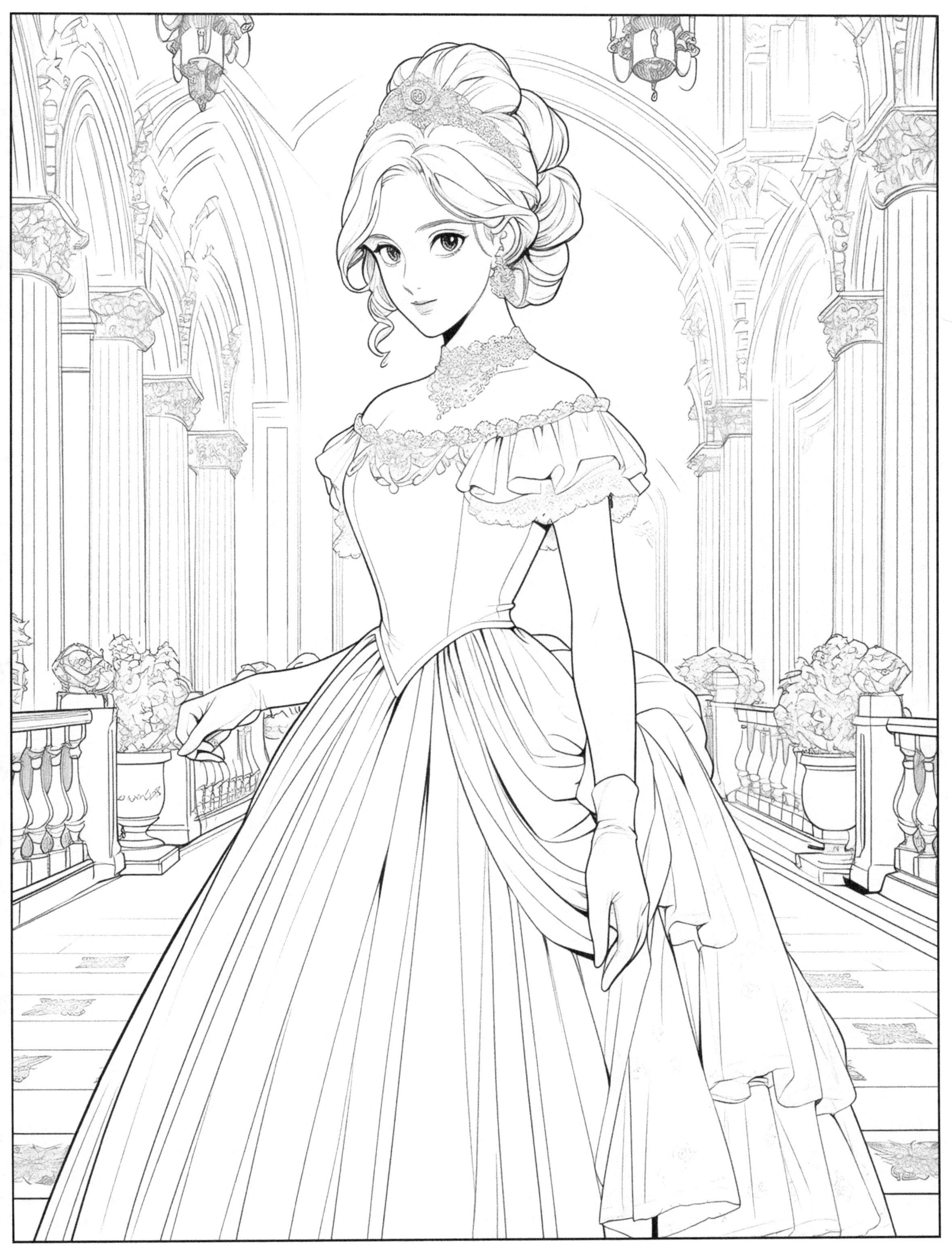

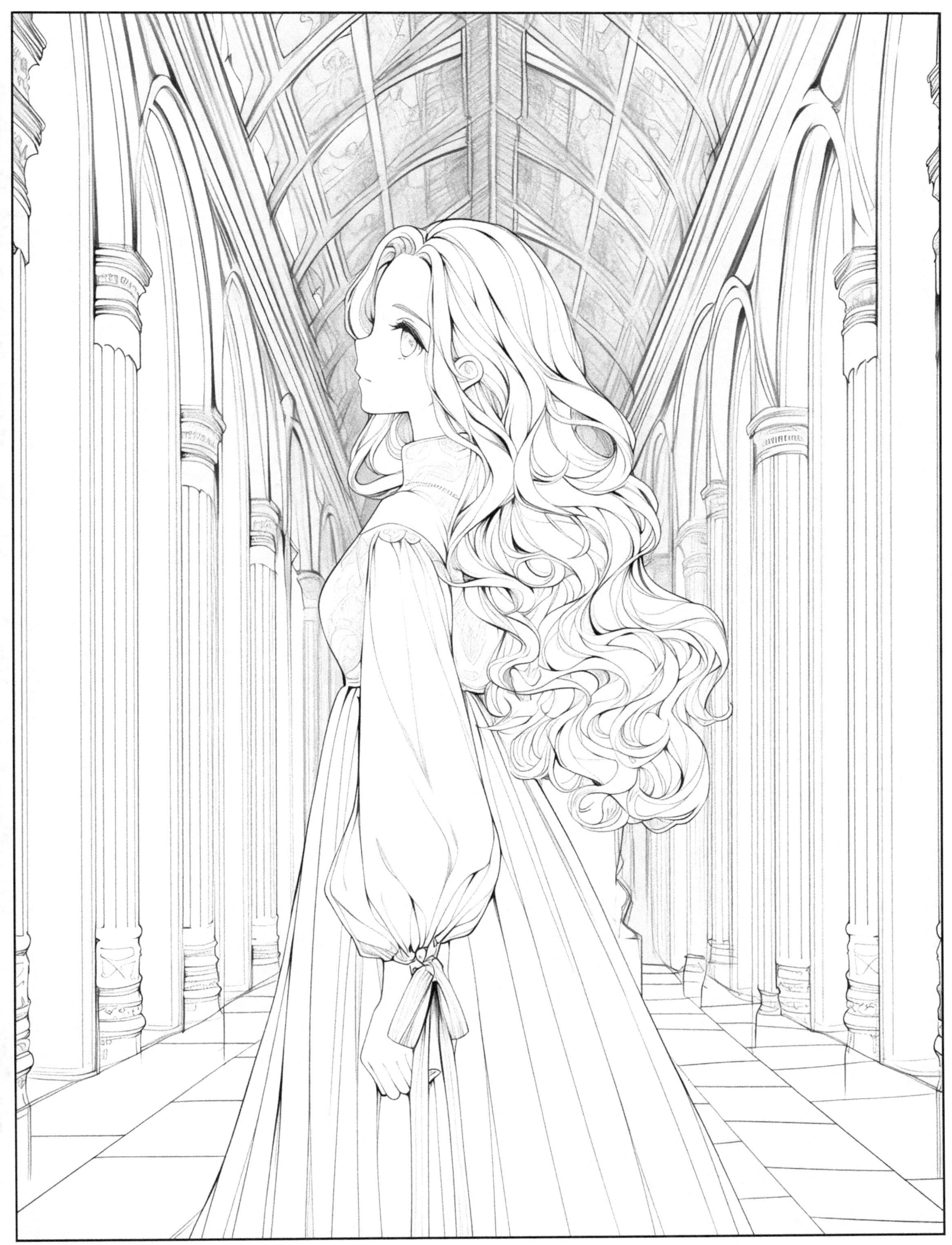

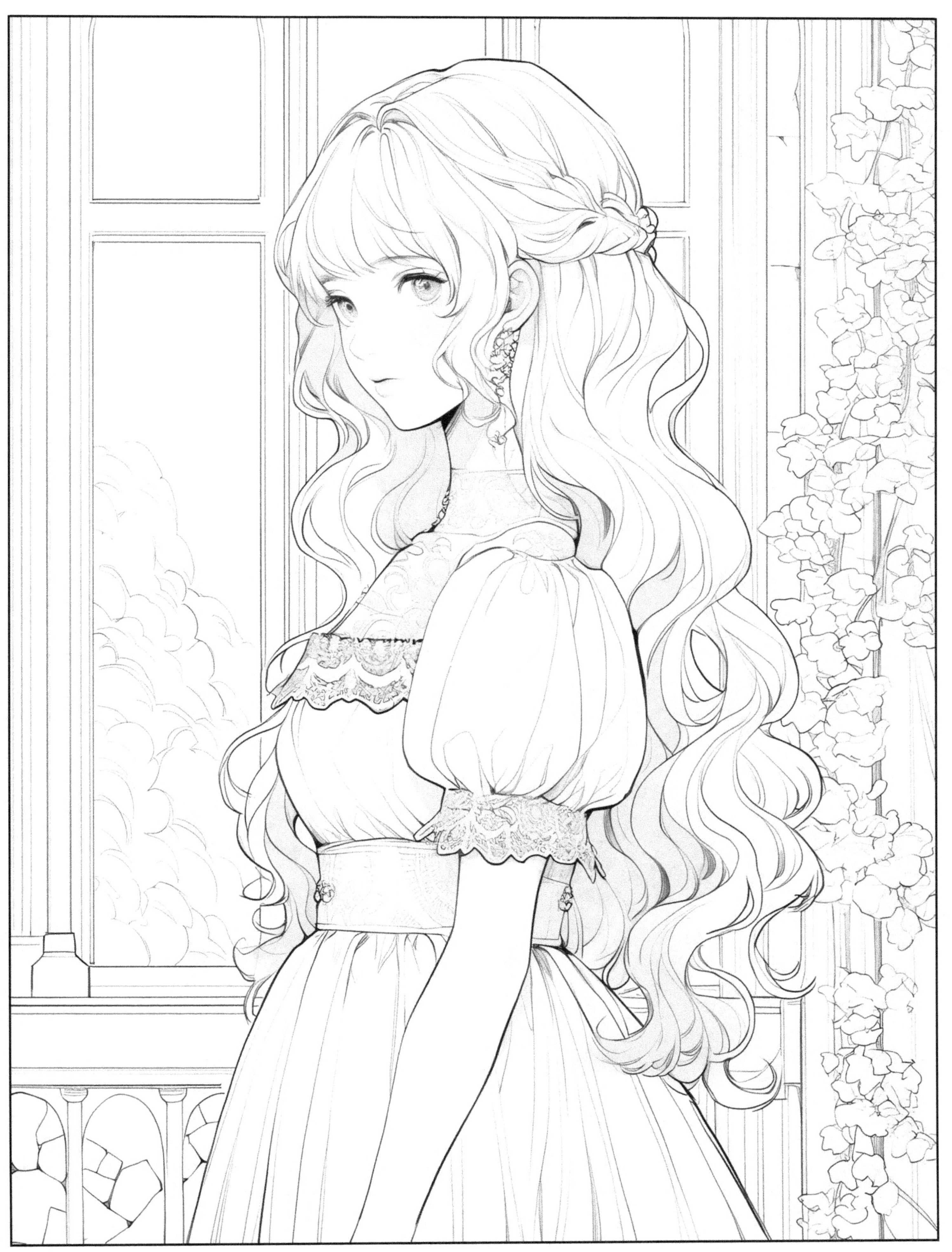

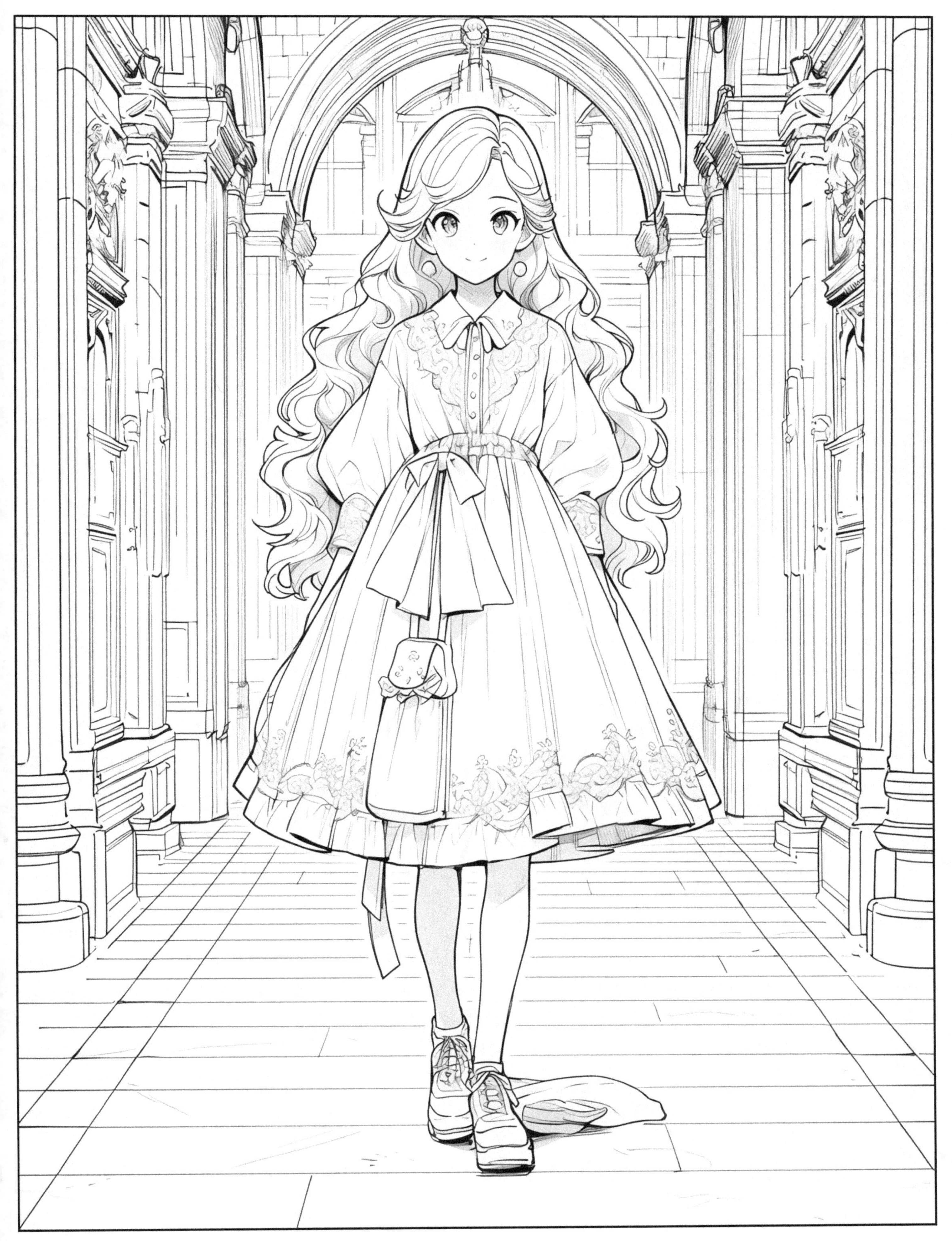

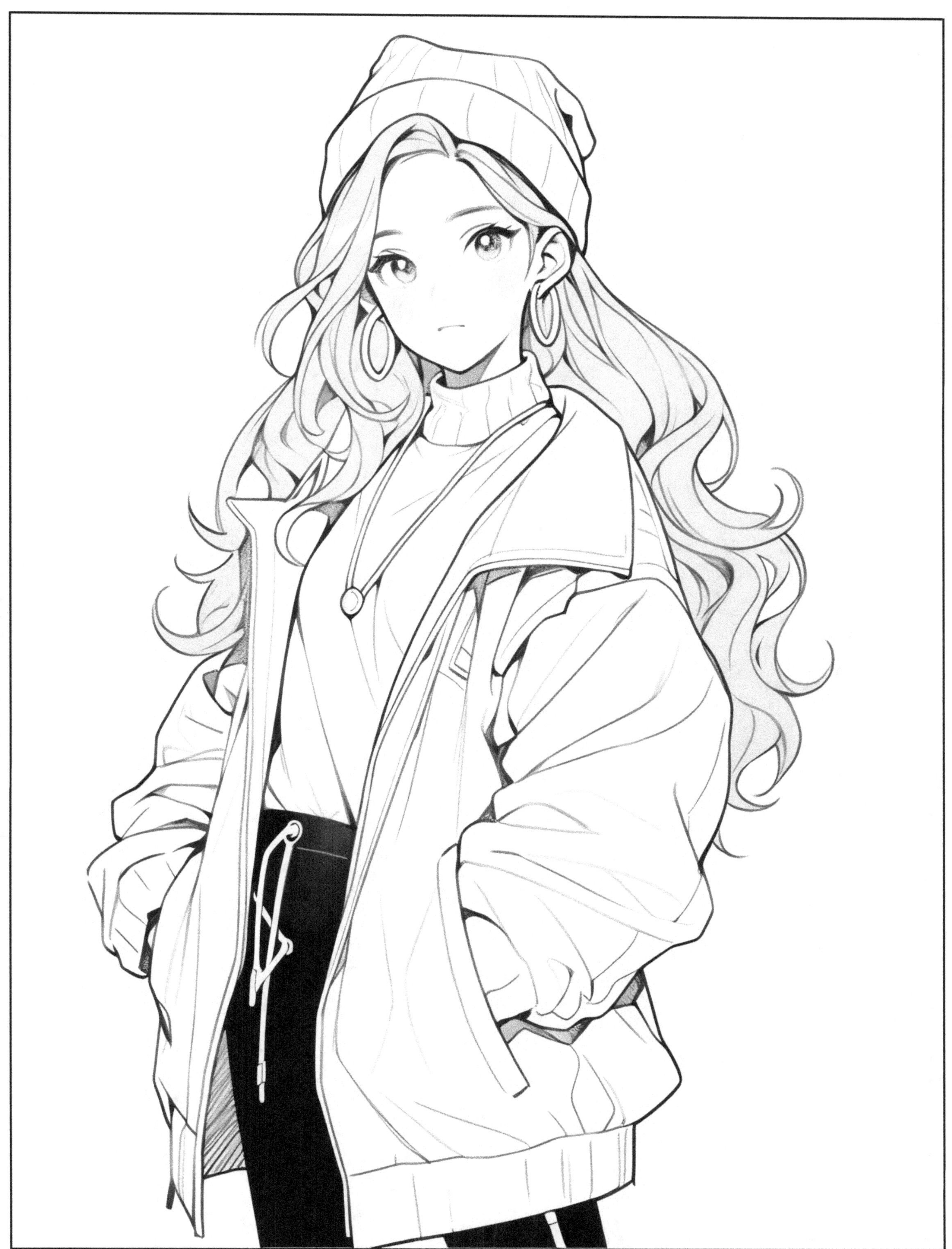

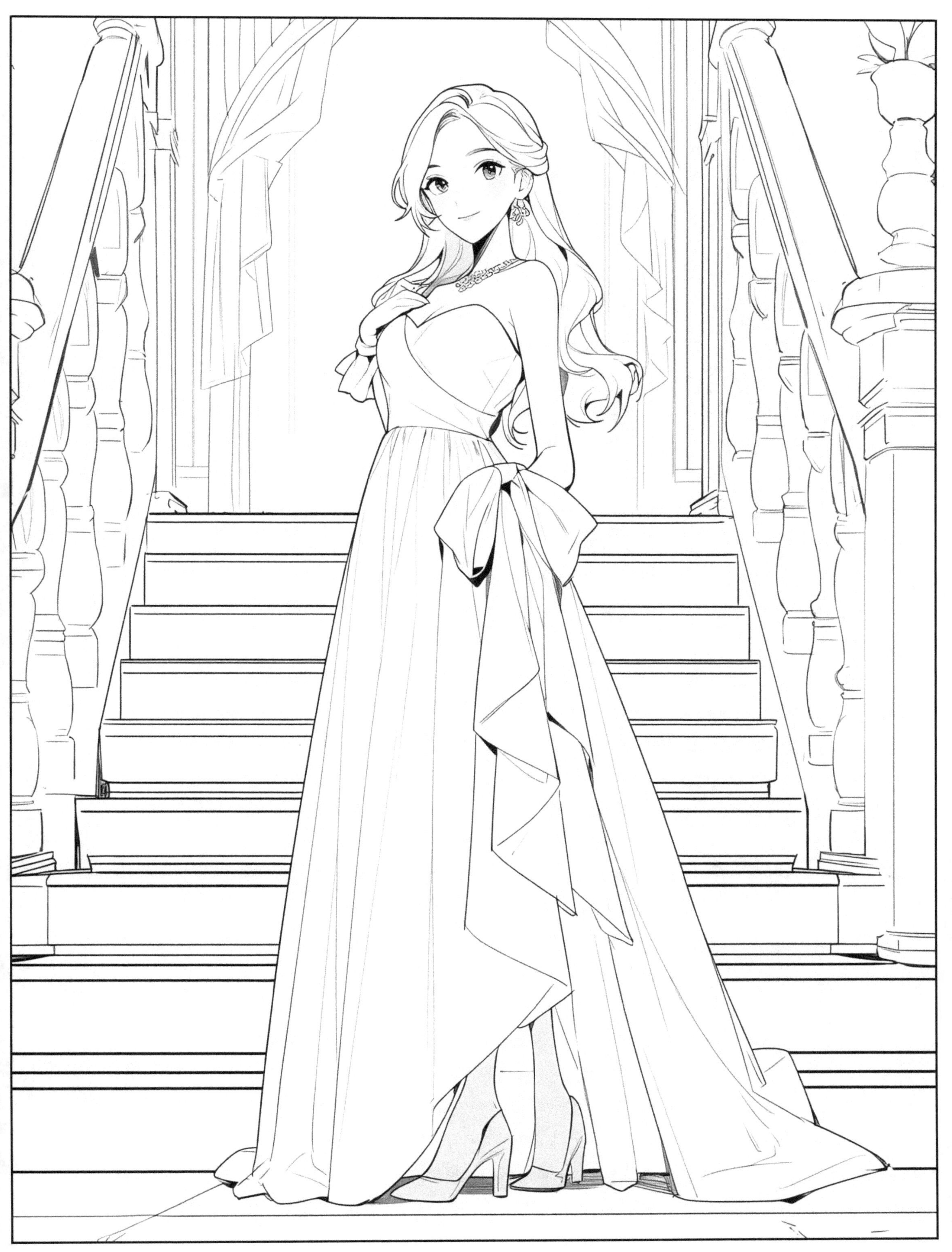

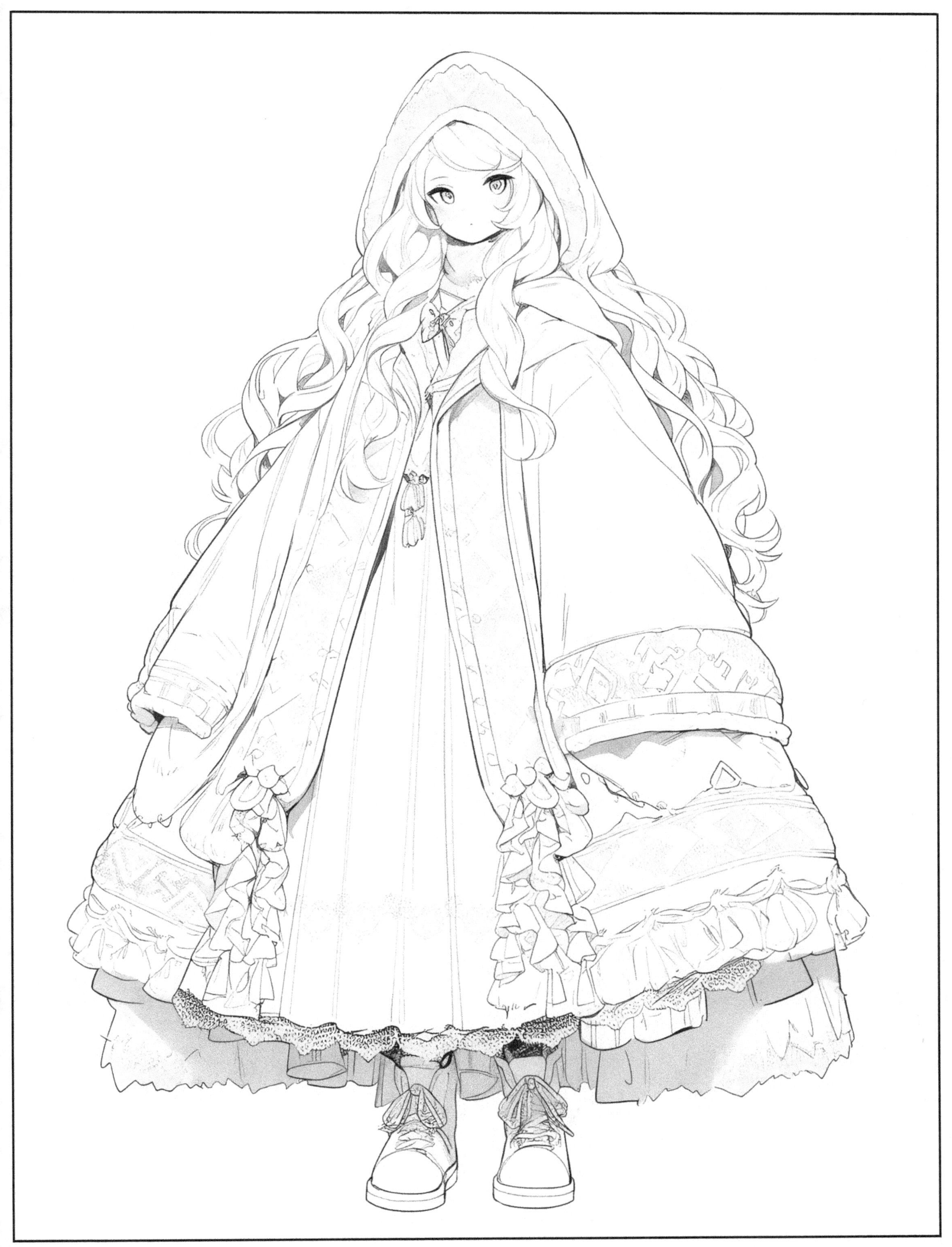

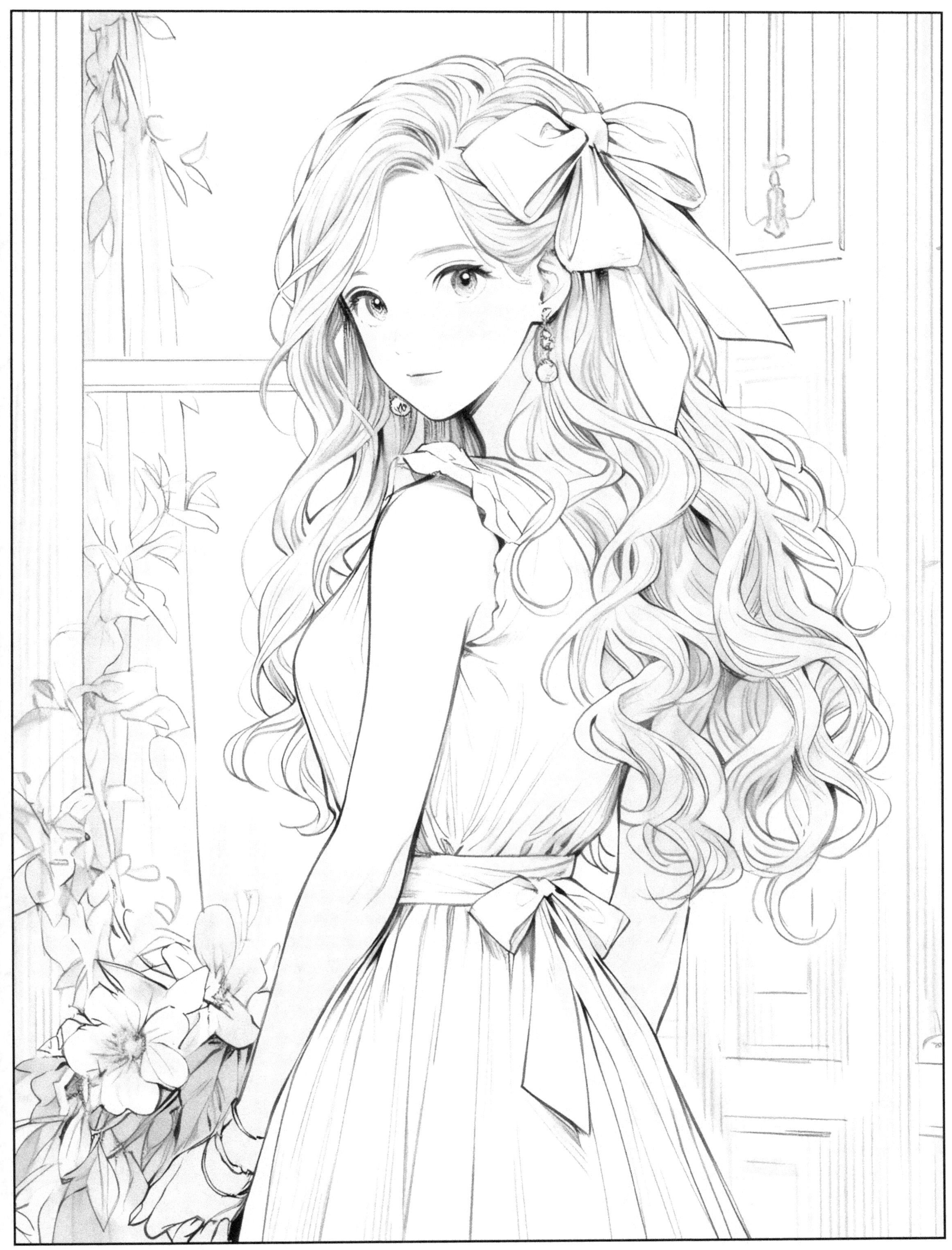

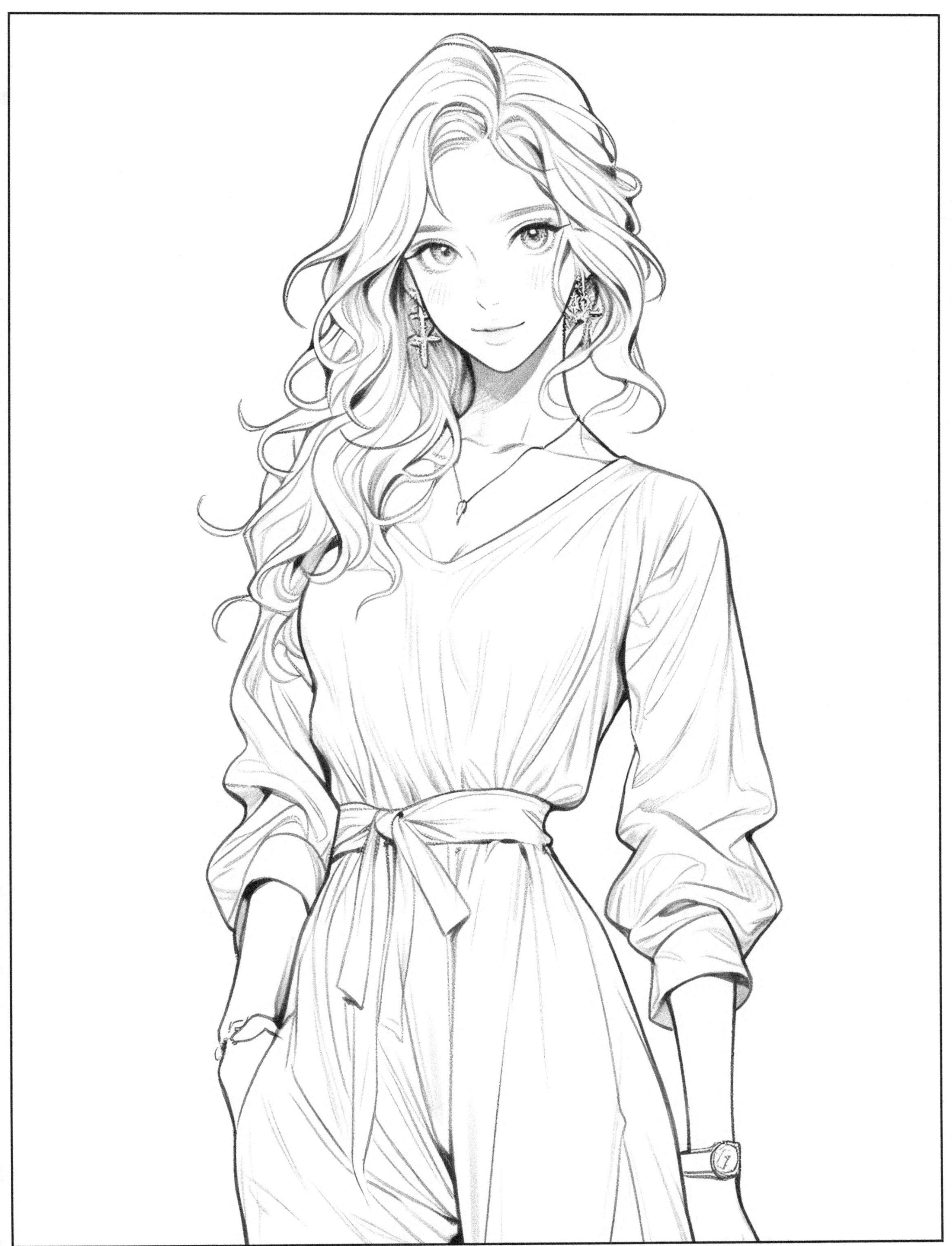

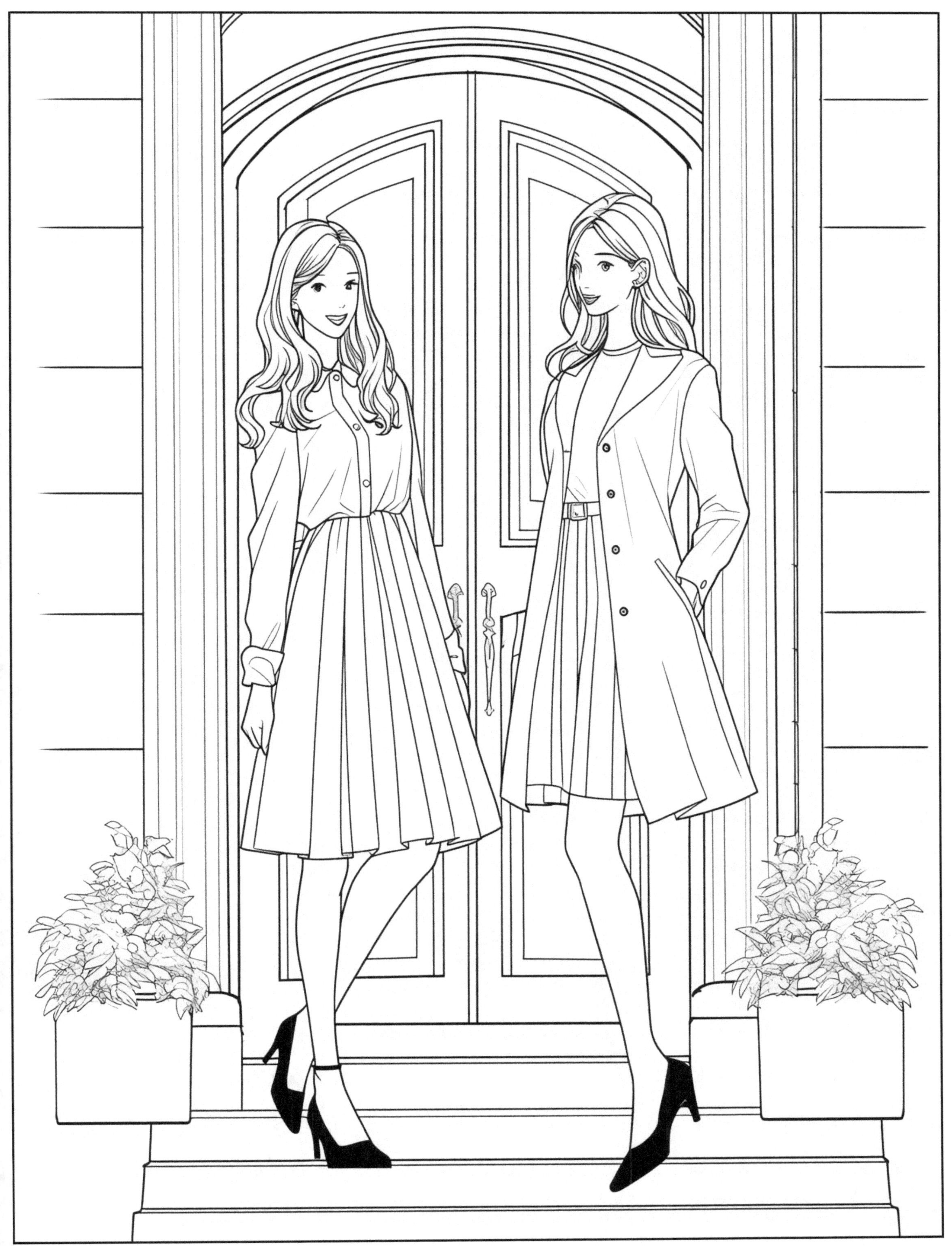

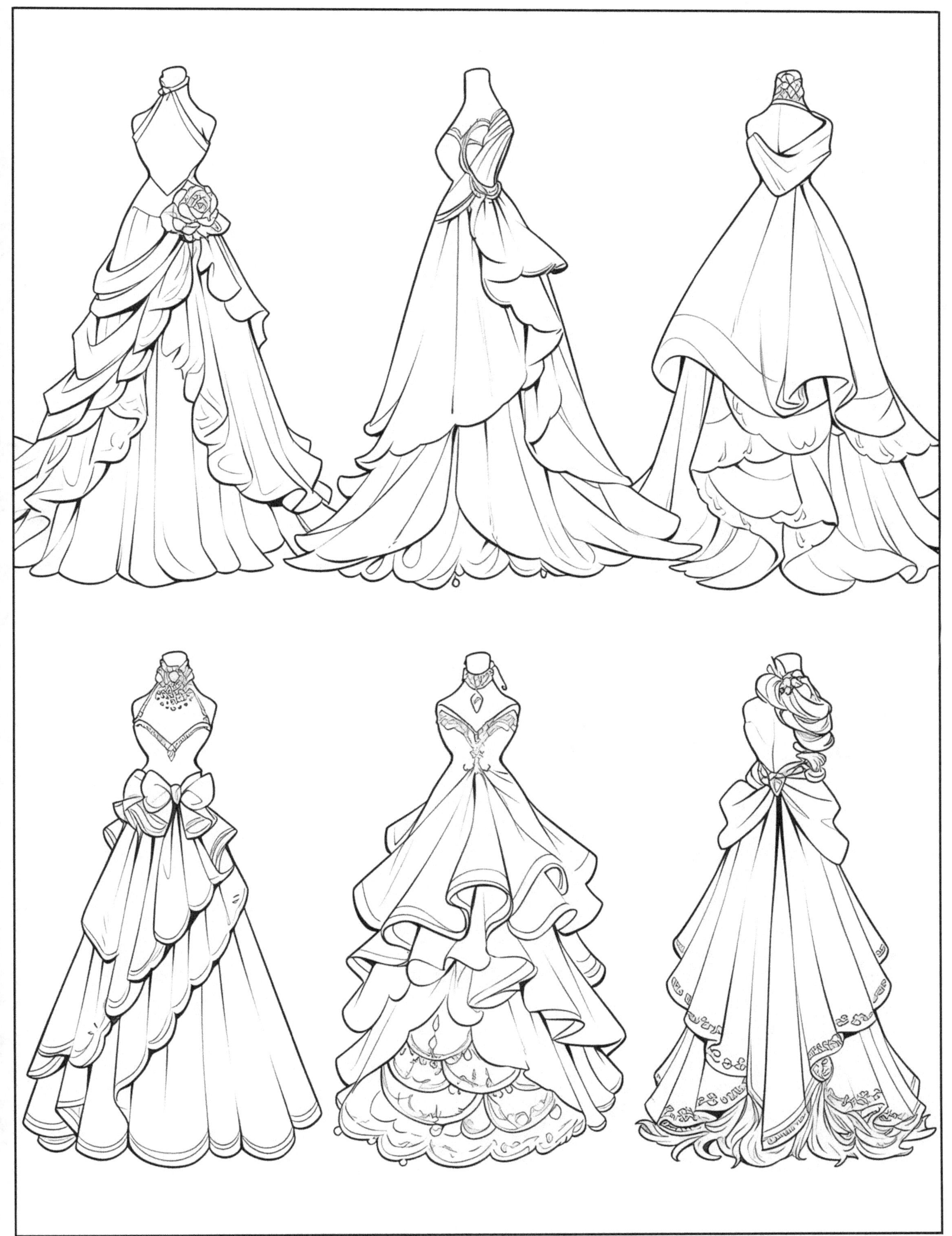

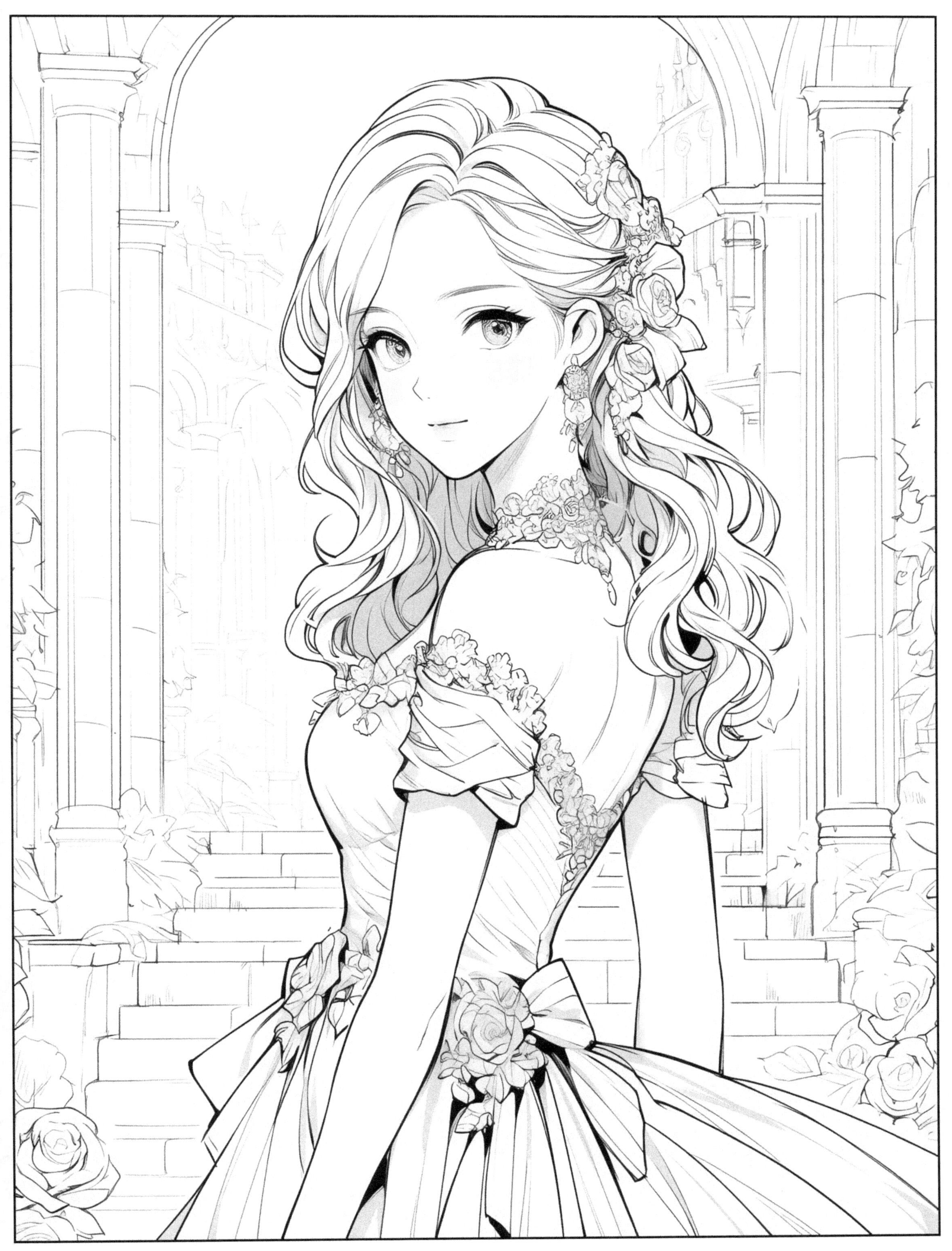

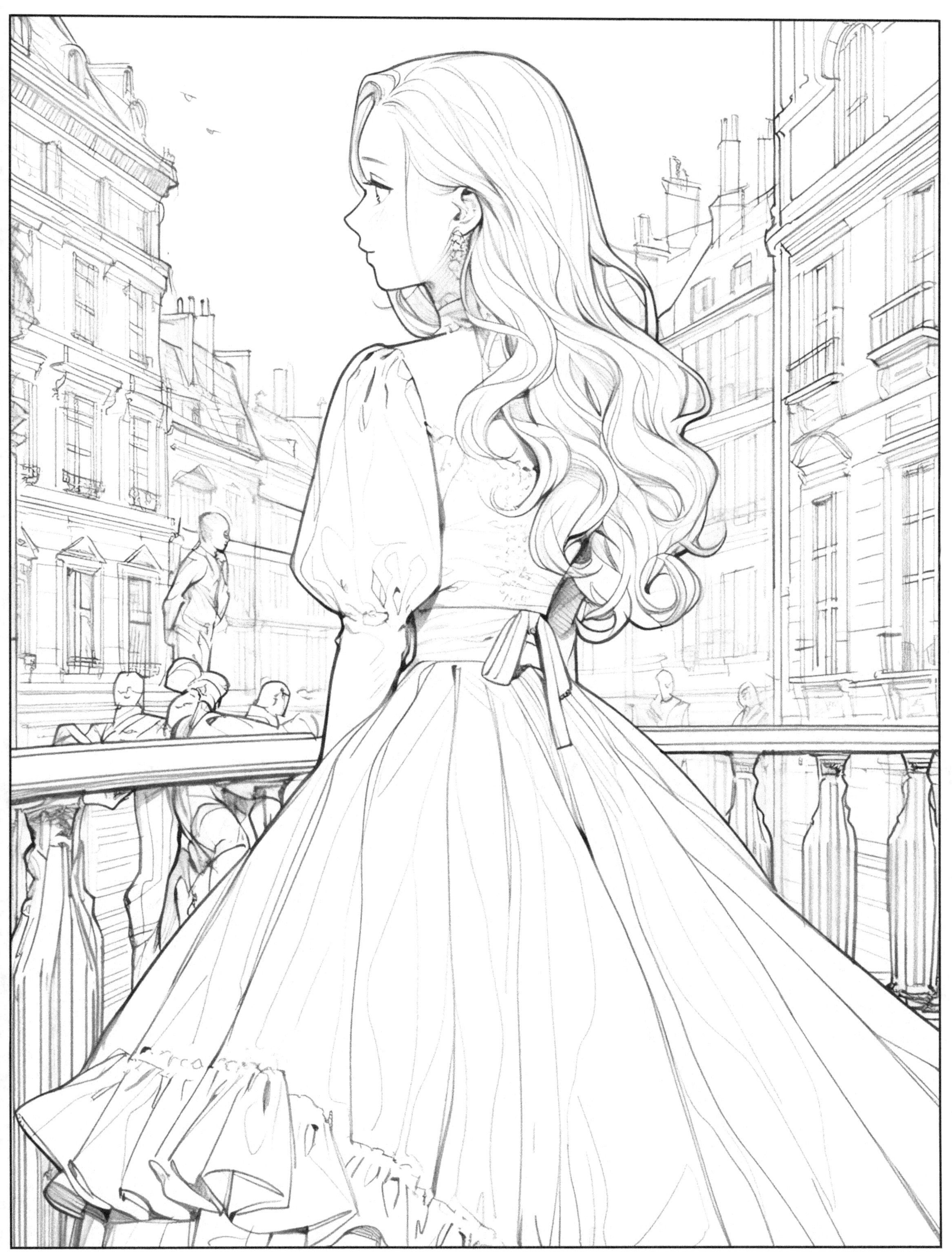

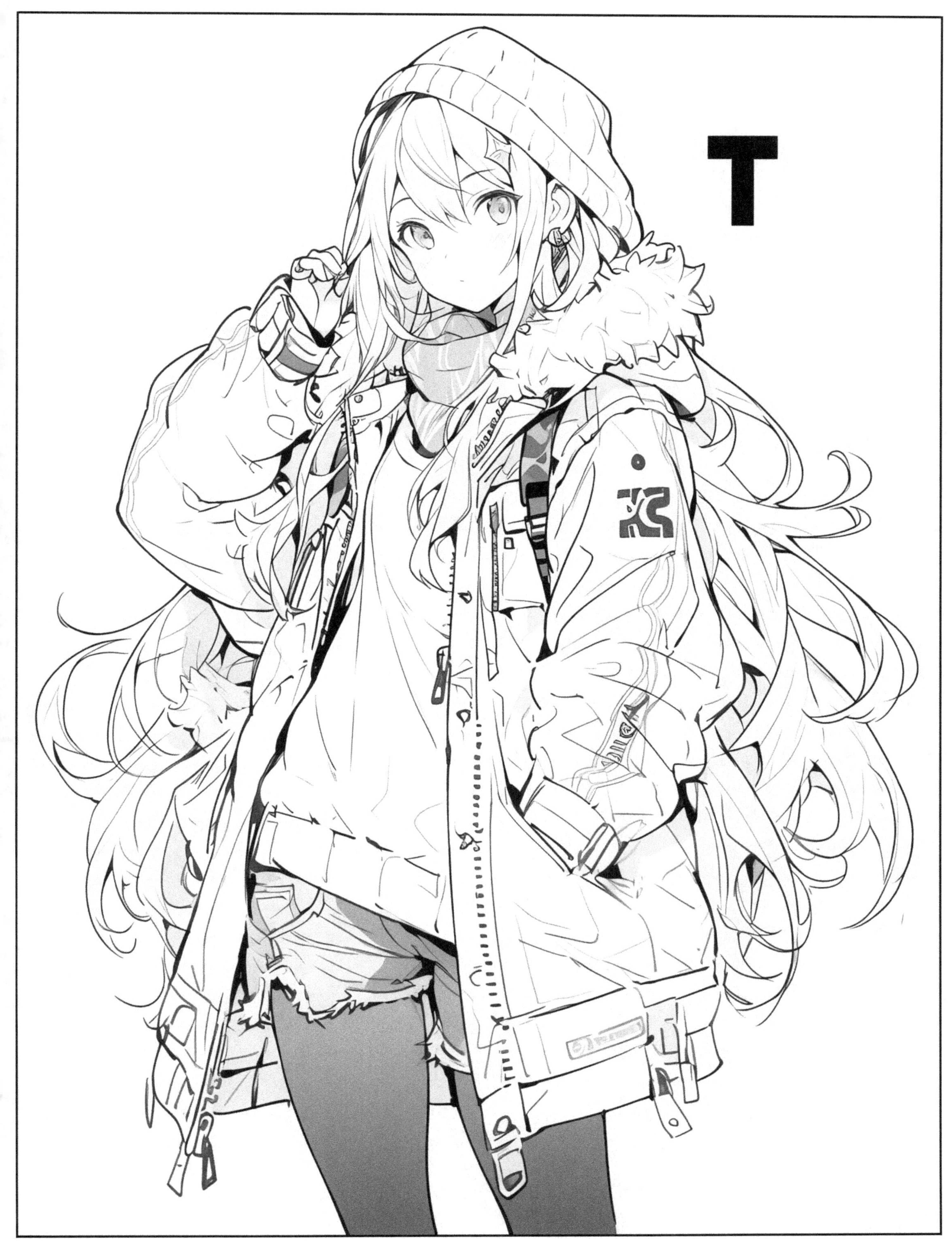
T

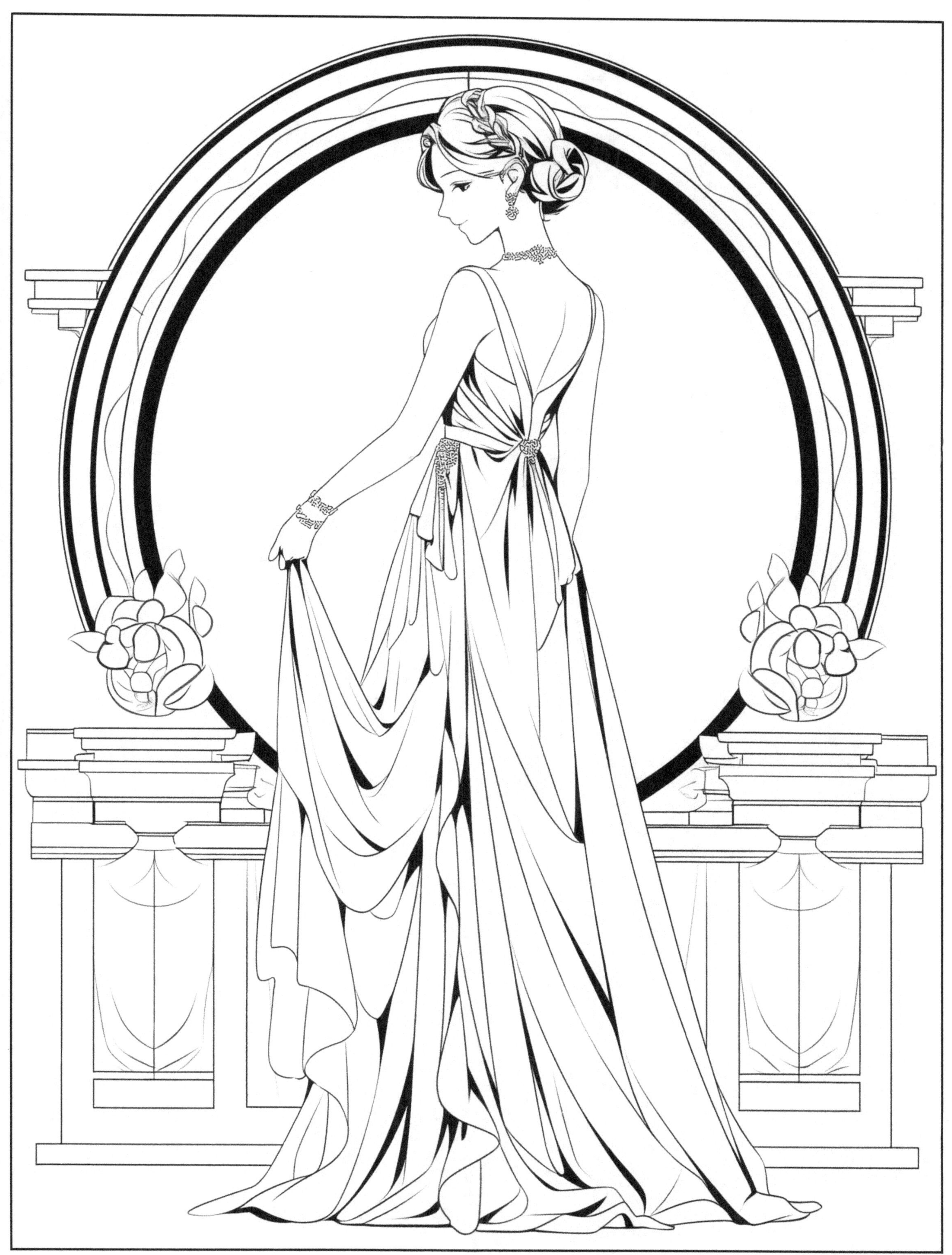

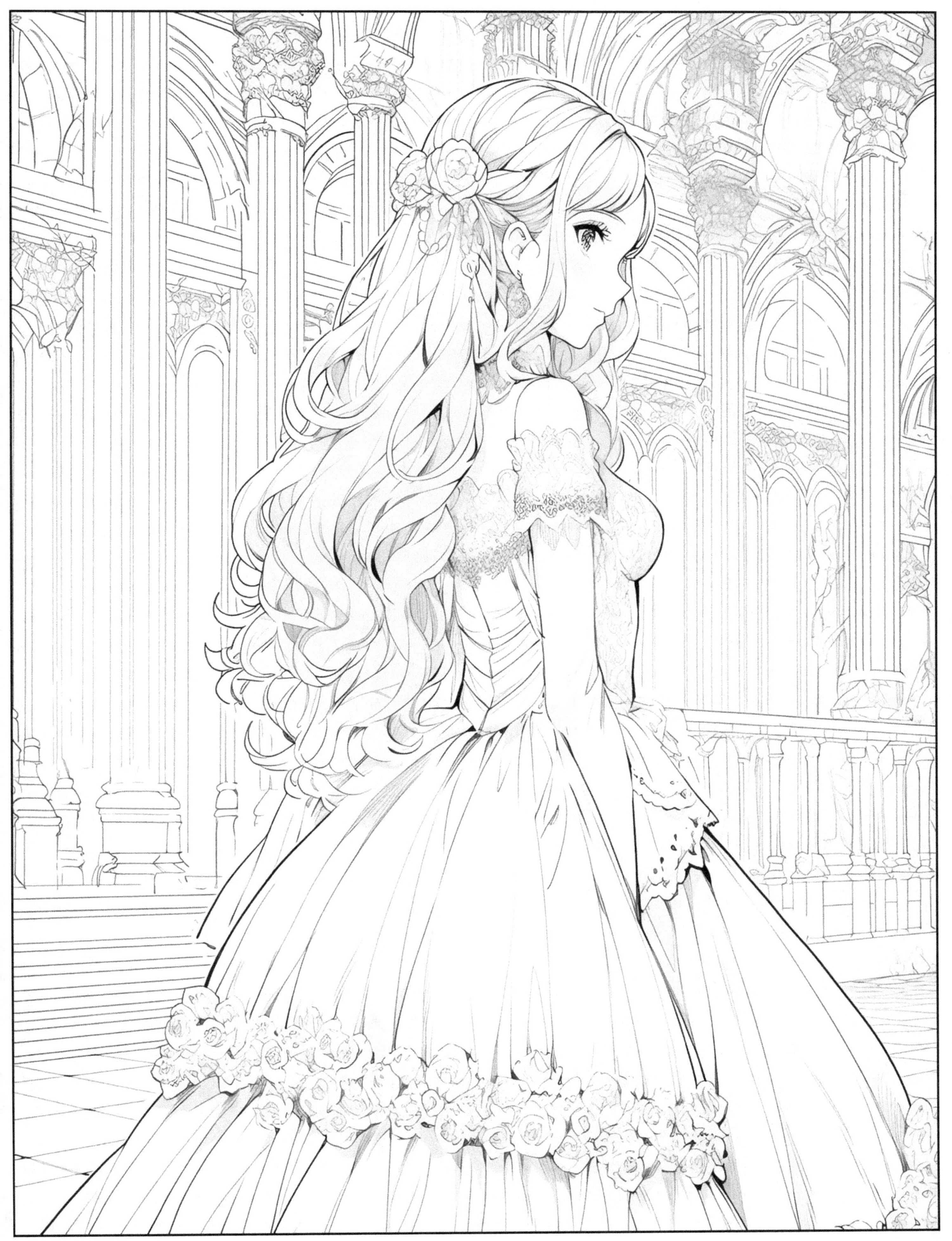

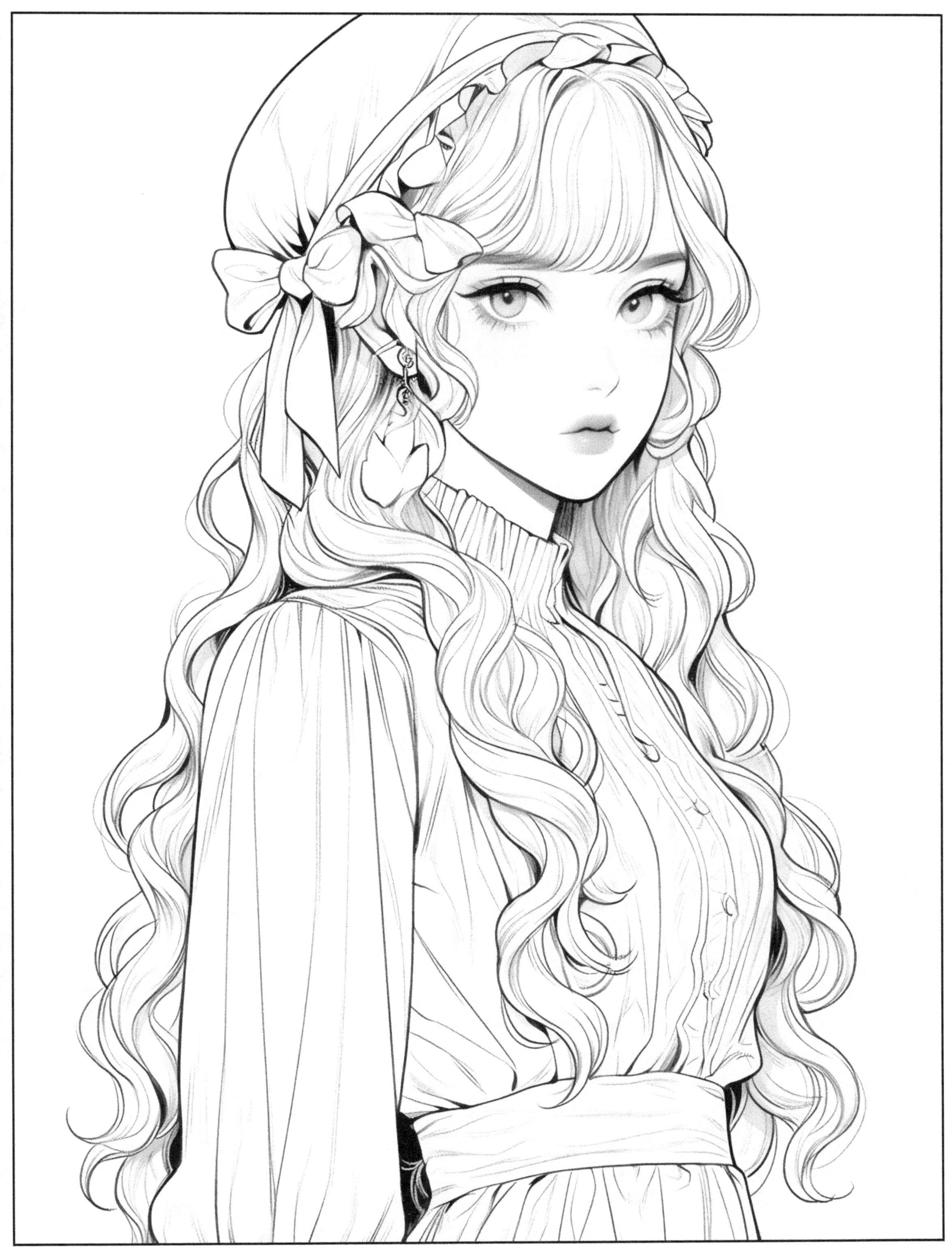

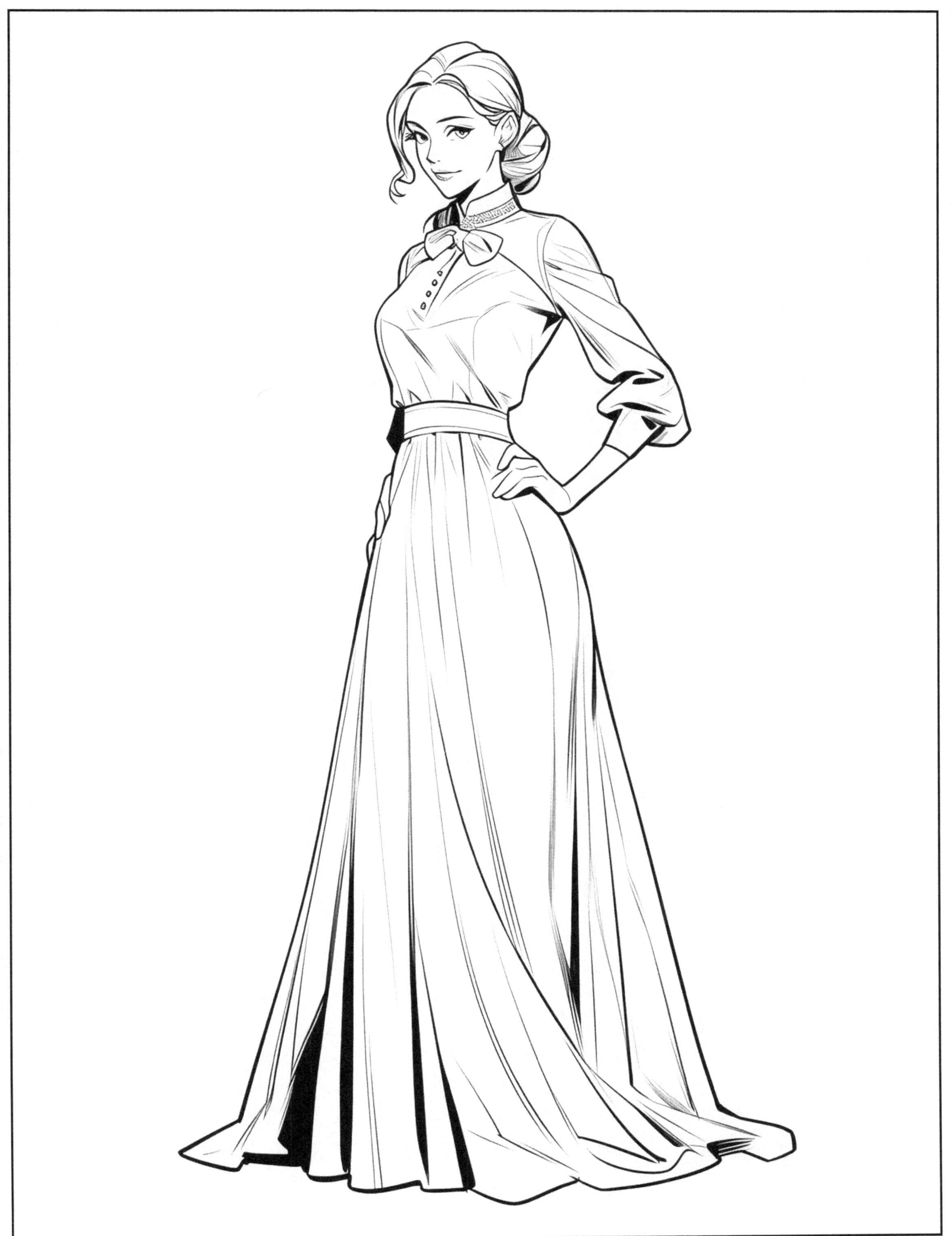

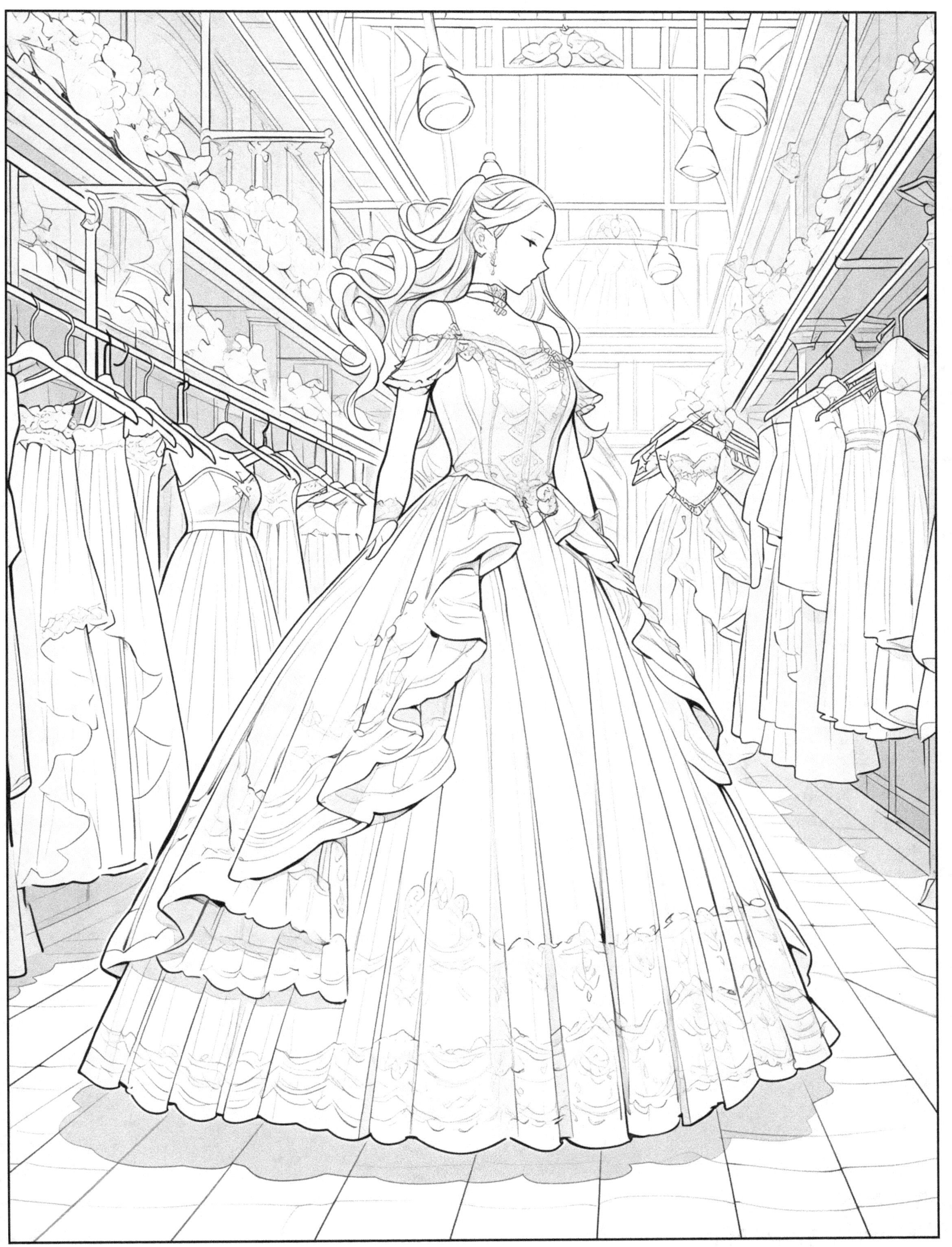